WHY NOT
PARLIAMENTARISM?

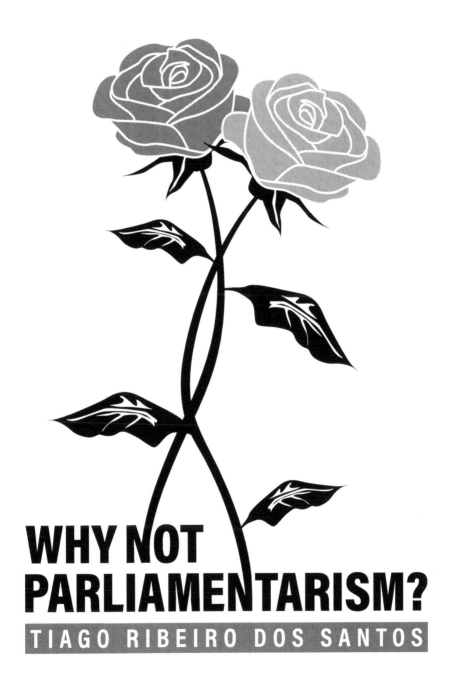

WHY NOT PARLIAMENTARISM?

TIAGO RIBEIRO DOS SANTOS

ISBN: 979-8-6627-2017-6

Published by Wordzworth
www.wordzworth.com

Keywords: Democracy types, Parliamentarism, Presidentialism, Development, Institutions

For Marcela

CONTENTS

ACKNOWLEDGMENTS

I benefited from many exchanges, comments, criticism, and encouragement from, in alphabetical order, Abdullah Aydogan, Philip Barrett, Geoffrey Brennan, Otaviano Canuto, Bryan Caplan, Matheus Cavallari, Rogério Farias, John Gerring, Alan Hamlin, Garett Jones, Fabio Kanczuk, Arend Lijphart, Richard McManus, Robin Pearson, João Francisco Pereira, Steven Pinker, Aaron Rosenberg, Jim Slaughter, Stefan Voigt, John Wilbanks, and Robert Wright. I also thank two anonymous reviewers for comments on an earlier version of this text.

I thank Antonn Park and Irina Langer for help with editing and references. I thank the librarians at the Joint Bank Fund Library who were extremely helpful with this research. Adriana Ciccone showed me how simple it is to get data from Google Ngram Viewer. The team at Wordzworth has done an excellent job.

Carlos Eduardo Gonçalves deserves more than an acknowledgment; he deserves an apology. My poor friend was forced to discuss so many of these arguments that at one point I had to promise him that I would not talk about parliamentarism when we met. Many of the arguments here derive from these exchanges.

If you feel that you and I discussed enough of these arguments that your name should be here, you are right. My limitation is that in the past few years I have talked about this with so many people that I could not possibly list them all here. I do thank everyone who helped make this possible.

Marcela, you had to put up with this too, and you put up with so much else. This is for you.

PREFACE

If you have picked up this book because you believe it will be a direct dialogue with *Why Not Socialism?* by Cohen (2009) and *Why Not Capitalism?* by Brennan (2014), let me tell you in the very first sentence that it is nothing of the sort. Those are philosophy books that use thought experiments to assess the relative flourishing potential of socialist and capitalistic systems. Cohen imagines the amount of sharing there would be in an ideal camping trip, wonders how his insights might generalize for society, and concludes with a general desirability of socialism. Brennan, on the other hand, argues that the TV show "Mickey Mouse Clubhouse," where the Disney characters live in a state of harmony perfectly compatible with private property and markets, illustrates how utopia is actually capitalist.

This book is not about utopia. It is about a system that exists and is never perfect but is very successful when given the chance. It is also not a thought experiment but an attempted defense of parliamentarism that is at the same time based on common sense, theory, and evidence. The reason it is called *Why Not Parliamentarism?* is to claim for the parliamentary project the same level of goodwill that so many other proposals enjoy. How can socialism, an idea that has failed so many times before (Niemietz, 2019), get to ask "why not?" Or capitalism, a concept that, when most vigorously defended, often translates into the defense of monopolistic or oligopolistic interests (Zingales, 2012), do it as well but not parliamentarism?

Cohen's and Brennan's works may well be no more than very carefully argued philosophy books and not meant to be taken as guides to action. As such, the books are very impressive and are both enjoyable to read. However, the fact that they may not be meant to be programmatic books does not stop people from acting on them or from acting on utopian arguments much like the ones presented in them. If "willingness to act" can be measured by the number of t-shirts that promote one of the projects, socialism and capitalism are doing fine, while parliamentarism is in the awkward situation of not having one single offer available in all of Google Shopping.[1] I came to believe that the text I was already writing, which until then was called "The Case for Parliamentarism," deserved to compete at that level.

Texts about parliamentarism are usually very academic in their jargon (this one suffers from that a little bit too, but I tried to minimize it). Unlike most policy texts, they are full of caveats and "further research is needed" admonitions and rarely make explicit judgment (this one does *not* suffer from that). Two outstanding exceptions are Linz and Valenzuela's (1994) books, *The Failure of Presidential Democracy*, volumes 1 and 2, and Selinger's (2019) *Parliamentarism*. Neither takes the approach of this book, however. I urge you to read those other texts, which I believe are complementary, but also read this one.

In a nutshell, my argument is that parliamentary systems of government are very likely responsible for a large share of the general increase in welfare indicators that have been observed since the 18th century. This relationship is supported by several factors. Parliamentary countries fare much better than non-parliamentary countries today in numerous dimensions, such as income, health, or press freedom. This increase in performance largely coincides with the changes toward parliamentary systems. Political science analysis of the different systems is close to a consensus on the superiority of parliamentarism, economic models almost unanimously point in the same direction, and empirical evidence supports it. Auxiliary evidence from local governments and private corporations lend even greater support. Through a Bayesian analysis that combines all of these pieces of evidence, I show that it is very likely that parliamentary systems are causally linked to better outcomes. Parliamentary does not come close to solving all of the problems in Public Choice theory, and such a claim would be preposterous. It only fares better than any other arrangement proposed until today.

---

[1] At least this was true on June 19, 2020. I wish this will change in the future, but I do not assign a large probability to that.

WHO IS THIS?

You are used to seeing this kind of book written by people who have published an entire bibliography on the subject. Their resumes speak for themselves. That is not my case, so I will have to speak on my behalf. To better explain why I became convinced I should write this, I will introduce a story I was first made aware of by Tim Harford.[2] I summarize it below from Ripley's (2009) account.

The Beverly Hills Supper Club fire, which occurred on May 28, 1977, was the third deadliest nightclub fire in the history of the US, with a total of 165 dead. Eighteen-year old Walter Bailey was working as a busboy on that day and was one of the first people to realize there was a fire. He saw the smoke behind the door and, exercising remarkable judgment, decided not to open the door that was still containing the fire. He urged his superiors to clear the space, but they were unphased. He then proceeded to the club stage and told all people present where the emergency exits were and that they should leave. Other members of the staff, however, did not take him seriously. With this, many in the public also ignored the pleas from the young man asking them all to leave. Bailey, however, was determined to help and made several trips in and out of the building. He was still able to save many people but always felt he could have done more, which is why he avoided giving interviews for some 30 years.

We wonder what makes us different from Walter Bailey. Why did he act? One thing we are told is he had a knack for science, and this type of knowledge prevented him from opening the door and making the disaster much worse. Another contributing factor was his detachment to the job, so he felt that the danger of being fired was nothing compared to the danger the people were facing. Surely pure randomness played its

---

[2]   https://timharford.com/2020/06/
       cautionary-tales-ep-9-fire-at-the-beverly-hills-supper-club/

part. But there is one crucial difference he has from the rest of us—he was there. He saw the fire; he was one of the first to see it. My point is that I am not a leading researcher in this topic, but I am in the metaphorical Supper Club.

I graduated in law in Rio de Janeiro in 2005. In 2007, I joined the Brazilian foreign ministry and worked with an array of countries and institutions, from Western Africa to the European Union to the United Nations to the G20. My knowledge about Brazilian institutions was complemented at the University of Chicago Harris School of Public Policy by an acquired knowledge of American institutions[3] and by empirical and theoretical methods. As of this writing, I am an advisor at the World Bank Board of Directors, where I have the chance to interact with some of the world's leading economists, both inside and outside the bank. Serendipity has ensured that I experienced firsthand some of the issues the paper deals with. I had the chance to be a monitor for the referendum for the independence of South Sudan and to see how serious the work is—something I deal with in the "What to do" chapter. When I mention below that all founding documents of development banks resemble each other, I can recall how I learned this fact from translating the agreement for the Asian Infrastructure Development Bank into Portuguese for internalization in Brazilian law.

Most important, however, was an invitation I received. My then supervisor, Otaviano Canuto, who was an executive director at the World Bank, asked if I would co-write a paper on the economic effects of the Brazilian Constitution. I thought it was a great opportunity and am proud of the article we published (Canuto and Santos, 2018). The research for the article led me to inquire more and more on the possible effects of systems of government. The question would be far too large for our article, though, so we did not include it there. But I have been researching it ever since, and this is the result.

---

[3] Much of it I got from Will Howell's classes, an author to whom I present several counterpoints in this text and one of the greatest teachers I have had. Shoulders of giants, as they say.

DISCLAIMER:

The opinions expressed in this book do not represent the views of the Brazilian Ministry of Foreign Affairs or of the World Bank Group. This not a peer-reviewed book. All errors are mine.

INTRODUCTION

One thing I learned from Pinker (2012) is that when you are going to defend a thesis that is both highly consequential and in defiance of common sense, you should conduct a "sanity check." This means assessing whether your thesis flies in the face of everything people know about the subject. In this book, I argue that parliamentary systems are vastly superior to presidential systems. The word "superior" is deliberately chosen because parliamentary systems outperform presidential ones in just about any aspect worth pursuing by a respectable and universal ethical philosophy. Not only are they more efficient and more protective of individual liberties, but they are also more equal. Parliamentary systems are more stable, are less prone to coups, and are also more adaptable and incorporate changes quicker than presidential systems. They preserve traditions yet also innovate, and they grow faster and better protect the environment.[4]

Parliamentary systems promote equal rights for all genders while allowing for better expression of the differences between genders. As Falk and Hermle (2018) say after observing 80,000 individuals in 76 countries, "the more that women have equal opportunities, the more they differ from men in their preferences." They are more democratic and less populistic and decrease the importance of religion[5] while still preserving the freedom of religion for the truly devoted.

These are bold claims indeed, so I should start the sanity check. Could it be possible that parliamentary systems are that much better? Most people, even development economists, believe that forms of government have little relation with the positive outcomes mentioned above.

---

[4]   These characteristics are discussed below. For innovation, see Cornell University, INSEAD, and WIPO (2019, p. xxxiv). For the environment, see *https://epi.yale.edu/epi-results/2020/component/epi*

[5]   See *https://www.pewforum.org/2018/06/13/how-religious-commitment-varies-by-country-among-people-of-all-ages/.*

In their view, many parliamentary countries succeed and fail, and many presidential countries succeed and fail, maybe with a slight edge in favor of parliamentary countries. This is a mistaken view. Considering that the number of parliamentary countries is very close to the number of presidential countries, let's do an exercise.

Before anything else, let us establish a general sense of parliamentary and presidential governments. In broad terms, a country is parliamentary when the government is appointed and dismissed by the legislature, and the ministerial cabinet has collective responsibility. It is presidential when the head of government is directly elected, is free to appoint and dismiss the ministers, and is ultimately responsible for government business. There are several deviations from these ideal types[6], and we will discuss this further below.

Moving on to the exercise. To start, I select a ranking of countries by gross domestic product (GDP) per capita, shown in table 0.1. The top 30 countries include oil-rich countries (Qatar, Brunei, Kuwait, UAE, Bahrain, and Oman), 2 presidential countries (the US and South Korea), and no less than 22 parliamentary countries.

Table 0.1 Countries by GDP per capita PPP, 2018

Rank	Country
1	Qatar
2	**Luxembourg**
3	**Singapore**
4	Brunei
5	**Ireland**
6	**Norway**

---

[6] In the name of consistency, following Brownlee (2009) when I have to classify, I rely on the Database of Political Institutions (using the latest data from Cruz, Keefer, Scartascini, 2017) to classify countries as presidential (0 in the system variable) or parliamentary (1 or 2 in the system variable) if they score above 3 in the Legislative Index of Electoral Competitiveness (LIEC) variable and the Executive Index of Electoral Competitiveness (EIEC), which means that there must be multiple candidates (even if there is only party). However, different studies use different definitions, typically requiring much higher levels of democracy. As discussed in Chapter 3, different definitions do not undermine the case.

Rank	Country
7	United Arab Emirates
8	Kuwait
9	**Switzerland**
10	*United States*
11	**San Marino***
12	**Netherlands**
13	Saudi Arabia
14	**Iceland**
15	**Sweden**
16	**Germany**
17	**Australia**
18	**Austria**
19	**Denmark**
20	Bahrain
21	**Canada**
22	**Belgium**
23	Oman
24	**Finland**
25	**France**
26	**United Kingdom**
27	**Malta**
28	**Japan**
29	*South Korea*
30	**Spain**

Parliamentary countries are in bold, and presidential countries are in italics. Names of countries that are neither presidential nor parliamentary are written in regular text. Source: International Monetary Fund (2018).

If one looks at life expectancy of United Nations (UN) countries, the results are similar.

Table 0.2 UN countries by life expectancy

Rank	Country
1	Monaco
2	**Japan**
3	**Singapore**
4	San Marino*
5	**Iceland**
6	Andorra*
7	**Switzerland**
8	*South Korea*
9	**Israel**
10	**Luxembourg**
11	**Australia**
12	**Italy**
13	**Sweden**
14	**France**
15	**Norway**
16	Liechtenstein*
17	**Canada**
18	**Spain**
19	**Austria**
20	**Netherlands**
21	**New Zealand**
22	**Belgium**
23	**Finland**
24	**Ireland**
25	**Germany**
26	**United Kingdom**
27	**Greece**
28	**Malta**
29	*United States*
30	**Denmark**

Source: CIA (2019)

Now, one might object that the two tables list the same countries. The richest parliamentary countries are also the parliamentary countries with greatest life expectancy. That is mostly true, but not completely (notice the absence of oil-rich countries in the second list), and is not obvious to many people.

In 2015, all countries represented at the UN unanimously adopted 169 Sustainable Development Goals (SDGs) targets. If it was clear to world leaders and public opinion that "all good things go together" around what Besley and Persson (2011) call "development clusters," perhaps instead of creating so many different targets, a more effective approach would have been to focus exclusively on one goal (e.g., economic growth), from which other good things would end up deriving. But in fact, there does not seem to exist a consensus on whether good things do indeed go together (Francis Fukuyama, for example, recently gave an interview calling into question precisely this idea[7]). What one could argue quite confidently is that "good things often, but not always, go together." For example, as proven by oil-rich autocracies, having a high GDP per capita would not necessarily lead to a freer, more open, and more tolerant country. Notice that a less than perfect, but general, relationship that good things go together is not a flaw in the argument but a prerequisite for its validity. If good things had no relationship to each other whatsoever, then it would be hard to claim that *any* societal arrangement is superior, parliamentary or not.

Sachs et al. (2018) produce the Sustainable Development Report (formerly the SDG Index & Dashboards), which is "the first worldwide study to assess where each country stands with regard to achieving the Sustainable Development Goals." They assess countries on the different goals and produce a final index. Below, I reproduce the full rank, once again marking in bold the parliamentary countries and in italics the presidential countries.

---

[7]   https://youtu.be/5R-dty5V9DM

Table 0.3 SDG Index Rank

Rank	Country
1	Sweden
2	Denmark
3	Finland
4	Germany
5	France
6	Norway
7	Switzerland
8	Slovenia
9	Austria
10	Iceland
11	Netherlands
12	Belgium
13	Czech Republic
14	United Kingdom
15	Japan
16	Estonia
17	New Zealand
18	Ireland
19	*Korea, Rep.*
20	Canada
21	Croatia
22	Luxembourg
23	*Belarus*
24	Slovak Republic
25	Spain
26	Hungary
27	Latvia
28	Moldova
29	Italy
30	Malta
31	Portugal

Rank	Country
32	*Poland*
33	*Costa Rica*
34	**Bulgaria**
35	*United States*
36	*Lithuania*
37	**Australia**
38	*Chile*
39	*Ukraine*
40	Serbia*
41	**Israel**
42	Cuba
43	**Singapore**
44	**Romania**
45	*Azerbaijan*
46	*Ecuador*
47	*Georgia*
48	**Greece**
49	*Uruguay*
50	*Cyprus*
51	*Kyrgyz Republic*
52	Uzbekistan
53	*Argentina*
54	China
55	**Malaysia**
56	*Brazil*
57	**Vietnam**
58	*Armenia*
59	Thailand
60	United Arab Emirates
61	**FYROM**
62	**Albania**
63	*Russian Federation*

Rank	Country
64	*Peru*
65	*Kazakhstan*
66	*Bolivia*
67	**Suriname**
68	*Algeria*
69	Montenegro*
70	**Trinidad and Tobago**
71	**Bosnia and Herzegovina**
72	*Paraguay*
73	*Tajikistan*
74	*Colombia*
75	*Dominican Republic*
76	*Nicaragua*
77	Morocco
78	*Tunisia*
79	**Turkey**
80	Bahrain
81	**Jamaica**
82	*Iran, Islamic Rep.*
83	Bhutan
84	*Mexico*
85	*Philippines*
86	*Panama*
87	Lebanon
88	*Cabo Verde*
89	*Sri Lanka*
90	**Mauritius**
91	Jordan
92	*El Salvador*
93	*Venezuela, RB*
94	Oman
95	*Mongolia*

Rank	Country
96	*Honduras*
97	*Egypt, Arab Rep.*
98	Saudi Arabia
99	*Indonesia*
100	*Gabon*
101	*Ghana*
102	**Nepal**
103	**Belize**
104	**Guyana**
105	Kuwait
106	Qatar
107	**South Africa**
108	Lao PDR
109	**Cambodia**
110	*Turkmenistan*
111	**Bangladesh**
112	**India**
113	Myanmar
114	*Namibia*
115	*Zimbabwe*
116	**Botswana**
117	*Guatemala*
118	*Senegal*
119	*Kenya*
120	*Rwanda*
121	*Cameroon*
122	*Cote d'Ivoire*
123	*Tanzania*
124	*Syrian Arab Republic*
125	*Uganda*
126	**Pakistan**
127	**Iraq**

Rank	Country
128	**Ethiopia**
129	*Zambia*
130	*Congo, Rep.*
131	*Guinea*
132	**Togo**
133	*Gambia, The*
134	*Mauritania*
135	**Lesotho**
136	*Burkina Faso*
137	Swaziland
138	*Mozambique*
139	*Djibouti*
140	*Malawi*
141	*Burundi*
142	*Mali*
143	*Sudan*
144	Angola
145	*Haiti*
146	Sierra Leone
147	*Benin*
148	*Niger*
149	*Liberia*
150	*Nigeria*
151	*Afghanistan*
152	Yemen, Rep.
153	Madagascar
154	*Congo, Dem. Rep.*
155	*Chad*
156	*Central African Republic*

Source: Sustainable Development Report

* Classification not available from the Database of Political Institutions

Other rankings paint a similar picture. In the "World Press Freedom Index" by Reporters Without Borders (2019), 25 of the top 30 countries are parliamentary, and that ranking's relationship with GDP per capita is much less obvious. For example, Jamaica is ranked sixth for having a free press, even though it is not a high-income country. In the Global Peace Index, 29 of the first 30 countries are parliamentary. Many of them are not particularly rich, such as Malaysia (16th place) or Botswana (30th place), which suggests that there are benefits of being parliamentary that are not completely derived from greater income.

Perhaps one of the best indicators of overall performance among countries is the UN Development Program's Inequality-Adjusted Human Development Index, which measures the equal access citizens have to employment, health care and education. In this index, only 2 of the top 30 countries are presidential, and none of the them are in the top 20. In fairness, this straight relationship does not always hold. For example, the Americas, land of presidentialism, seem to perform relatively better in a measure of racial tolerance[8]—but the same measure also suggests a pattern of old societies being less tolerant than new societies (parliamentary New Zealand and Australia seem to do well, for example).

Until now, I have only provided snapshots of countries at their current state. Does a look at history suggest a similar story? It does. The "Great Escape," in the expression used by Deaton (2013) for the unprecedented rise in well-being, coincided with another historical turn: "The Industrial Revolution, beginning in Britain in the eighteenth and nineteenth centuries, initiated the economic growth that has been responsible for hundreds of millions of people escaping from material deprivation. The other side of the same Industrial Revolution is what historians call the 'Great Divergence,' when Britain, followed a little later by Northwestern Europe and North America, pulled away from the rest of the world." As it turns out, Northwestern Europe and North America[9] also followed

---

[8]   *https://www.washingtonpost.com/news/worldviews/wp/2013/05/15/a-fascinating-map-of-the-worlds-most-and-least-racially-tolerant-countries/*

[9]   The US stands out as an exception because it is not parliamentary, but it is no exception in terms of strong governmental accountability to the parliamentary body, as discussed below.

Britain "a little later" in adopting procedures that made the government increasingly accountable to parliament (Congleton, 2010).

A leading explanation for the Great Enrichment—McCloskey's term for basically the same process—is the new institutionalist view that the Glorious Revolution was the most important step in the process because of how it improved the protection of property rights. But this view seems curious. As McCloskey (2010) notes, "numerous societies—in fact, all of them, or else they are not societies but wars of all against all—have produced rules of property." She writes that "it was not property rights that the Dutch transferred to the English. Both the Dutch and the English had them anciently." What the Dutch transferred was a model based on the power of parliament.[10] Why is this then not the preferred causal hypothesis?

The phenomenon of the parliamentarization of Europe easily escapes many analysts because it was a gradual process (Von Beyme, 2000; Congleton, 2010) and is often confused with democratization. Von Beyme (2000), however, stresses that "what Huntington has called 'democratization' was at best parliamentarization, and this began during the French Revolution (from 1791). There were few waves of democratization in Europe in the 19th century." We have been using the same name for different phenomena. When the proper terms are used, parliamentarization for the expansion of parliamentary powers and democratization for the expansion of suffrage, it becomes clear that the first term is associated with general institutional improvements, while the latter does not have as much evidence in favor of it (in addition to the efficiency it provides in selecting representatives).

So European countries were the first to industrialize and were the first to become parliamentary. But they also share several other characteristics besides strong parliaments. If we examined the process only among European countries, would we find similar results? The answer is yes. As De Pleijt and Van Zanden (2016) show, parliaments developed

---

[10]   Congleton (2010) claims that the Glorious Revolution was a reassertion of parliamentary powers on a higher level. Even with this caveat, the point still holds: the revolution had the assertion of parliamentary power as its central characteristic.

unequally in the continent. They started in Spain but retreated from there and then developed in Britain and the Netherlands. These "differences in institutional development help to explain the economic divergence between northwestern and central Europe." In both a global and regional level, the first countries to adopt parliamentary systems did better earlier.

You may be itching to shout at me, "correlation is not causation." Indeed, it is not, and I have not even run a proper correlation test yet. The point here was to conduct a sanity check. Correlation may not be causation, but the existence of a true correlation (in the sense that it is not just a coincidence) between A and B implies one of three things: either A causes B, B causes A, or some C causes both A and B. This may sound trivial, but it is a point very often missed when these facts are discussed. If there is indeed a correlation between parliamentary systems and good outcomes broadly defined, then we are left with only three hypotheses: parliamentary systems foster good outcomes, good outcomes foster parliamentary systems, or something else fosters both.

The hypothesis seems to have passed the sanity test. There is now, at the very least, a hint of a pattern that deserves a more thorough investigation. But this is going to be an uphill battle. Development economists rarely agree on anything, but there is at least one set of beliefs that comes close to unanimity among them: (i) development is very hard, (ii) it must come from within the country, (iii) there is no one-size-fits-all solution, and (iv) any attempt at systematizing a path to is futile at best and downright evil at worst. I call this set of beliefs the "strict mystery" theory of development, according to which the causes of development are not only unknown but are also effectively unknowable, much like the mysteries of Catholicism. Even people proposing policies who objectively contradict the strict mystery theory usually pay lip service to this credo. I will be upfront and deny it.

The structure of the book is as follows. Chapter 1 makes the case for parliamentary systems, with both theoretical and empirical arguments. Chapter 2 discusses the "strict mystery" objections to what can be perceived as a "boilerplate solution." Chapter 3 examines definitional issues of presidential and parliamentary systems. Chapter 4 examines an alternative hypothesis for the patterns we are observing, and Chapter 5 provides a Bayesian estimate of how likely it is that the hypothesis of the great advantage of parliamentary systems is true. Chapter 6 asks what can be done.

1

The Case for Parliamentarism

I take two approaches to make the case for parliamentarism: examining the theories and examining the empirical evidence, from different sources. While none of the theories and evidence in isolation would be enough, we will see that they all converge in favor of parliamentary systems in a convincing manner. This convergence is made clearer in Chapter 5, which provides an estimate of the probability of the hypothesis. For simplicity, I compare parliamentarism only to its democratic alternative, presidentialism, given that democracy is "the only game in town" (Linz and Stepan, 1996).

1.1 Theory

As Rodrik (2015) writes in *Economics Rules*, there is no one true model for any given economic phenomenon. There are multiple models with different premises, but "[t]he applicability of a model depends on how closely critical assumptions approximate the real world," where critical assumptions are those that if modified "in an arguably more realistic direction would produce a substantive difference in the conclusion produced by the model." To assess the relative advantages of parliamentary versus presidential systems, I look into the multiple examinations of the issue and see how changing premises in a more realistic direction affects the conclusion.

1.1.1   Informal theory

From an informal theory perspective, the most influential thinker on the benefits of parliamentary systems has been Linz (1990, 1994). I could not summarize his thesis better than Lijphart (2008), so I will not try:

> *The first problem of presidentialism is what Linz calls "dual democratic legitimacy." In parliamentary systems, only the legislature is popularly elected and is the clear and legitimate representative of the people, but in presidential systems both president and legislature are popularly elected and are both legitimate representatives of the people—but it is quite possible and even likely that the president and the majority of legislators have divergent political preferences, even if they nominally belong to the same party. There is no democratic principle to resolve such disagreements. The practical result tends to be stalemate—and a strong temptation for the president to assume extraordinary powers or for the military to intervene. The second problem is "rigidity": presidents are elected for fixed periods of time, which can often not be extended because of term limits, even if a president continues to be popular and successful, and which cannot be shortened even if a president proves to be incompetent, or becomes seriously ill, or is beset by scandals of various kinds. Impeachment may be a possibility, but this process is almost always both very time-consuming and ultimately unsuccessful because extraordinary majorities are required to effect removal.*

> *The third serious problem is the "winner take all" nature of presidential elections. The winning candidate wins all of the*

executive power that is concentrated in the presidency, and it is "loser loses all" for the defeated candidate who often ends up with no political office and may disappear from the political scene altogether. He recognizes that parliamentary elections can be majoritarian, too, and he therefore adds: "Although parliamentary elections can produce an absolute majority for a single party, they more often give representation to a number of parties. Power-sharing and coalition-forming are fairly common, and incumbents are accordingly attentive to the demands and interests of even the smaller parties" (Linz 1990, p. 56). This is an important qualification because it means that his preferred type of parliamentary government is not British-style democracy with plurality elections and a two-party system but the kind of parliamentarism based on elections by proportional representation and multiparty systems that can be found in Germany, Sweden, and other Continental European democracies. This is also clearly my own preference.

The fourth serious drawback of presidentialism is that presidential election campaigns encourage the politics of personality—with an emphasis on the personal weaknesses and alleged character flaws of the candidates—instead of a politics of competing parties and party programs. In representative democracy, parties provide the vital link between voters and the government. Seymour Martin Lipset (2000) rightly calls political parties "indispensable" in democracies. The democratic ideal is to have strong and cohesive parties with clear programs. Anything that detracts from this ideal detracts from the viability of democracy.

There are, however, scarcely few explicit theoretical defenses of presidentialism. As Linz (1994) notes, most arguments in favor of presidentialism involve 1) invoking the tradition of countries that are already presidential, 2) arguing that presidential systems can be reformed in such a way that makes them closer to parliamentarism, 3) defending semi-presidential systems, or 4) proposing some innovative solution.

This is valid also of authors who wrote responses to Linz's arguments. Mainwaring and Shugart (1997), for example, write that "although we are not advocating presidentialism, we have argued that critics of presidentialism have overstated the degree to which this regime type is inherently flawed." Shugart and Carey (1992) argue that presidential systems can work well as long as the president is weak. That is hardly an argument in favor of presidentialism. Indeed, none of these responses suggest that presidentialism per se is a superior alternative to parliamentarism.

When looking for a principled defense of presidential powers, one could turn to Howell and Moe's (2016) *Relic*, which has a suggestive subtitle: *How Our Constitution Undermines Effective Government—and Why We Need a More Powerful Presidency*. Even here, however, the authors assert their belief that parliamentary systems are better than presidential systems in general. However, since they believe parliamentary democracy is not a realistic option for the US (they call it a "pie-in-the-sky" idea), the next best action would be to increase presidential powers instead of keeping the divided system they observe.

Before addressing Howell and Moe's arguments, however, it is important to make a clarification. The study of presidential systems is teeming with confusion because the most studied presidential system, the US, is very atypical. Presidential powers in the US are severely more limited than in other presidential countries. In general, there are two main sources of power for presidents: appointment to (and removal from) office and legislative power. Carey (2012) estimates that US presidents need Senate approval for around 1,200 to 1,400 of their appointed positions and for the most important ones. In other presidential countries, presidents are free to name whomever they want, not only for ministry positions but also to manage powerful state-owned enterprises. There usually are a few positions that depend on some form of parliamentary approval (most commonly Supreme Courts seats), but these are the exception.

US presidents also have atypically weak legislative powers. In the US, the main source of formal power is vetoing a bill—only in its entirety—which can be revoked by Congress with a qualified majority. In other countries, however, presidents may have exclusive constitutional agenda-setting powers on important issues (e.g., the budget); power for partial, and hence more flexible, vetoes; decree power (which amounts to unilateral legislation); and urgent requests.

The traditional weakness of the executive branch in the US, compared to other executive branches around the world, is very clearly demonstrated by Tocqueville (1838). In his classic text, *Democracy in America*, the French author describes how the American Congress can keep the government working in spite of the president's actions. European kings of his time, however, necessarily had to be involved in all government matters. In other words, an American president who loses the majority in Congress may stay in his position with relatively few problems for Congress. If a European king was not in agreement with parliament, however, a crisis would necessarily ensue:

> *It is an established axiom in Europe that a constitutional King cannot govern when the opinion of the legislative chambers is not in agreement with his.*
>
> *Several Presidents of the United States have been seen to lose the support of the majority of the legislative body, without having to leave power, nor without causing any great harm to society.*
>
> *I have heard this fact cited to prove the independence and strength of the executive power in America. A few moments of reflection are sufficient, on the contrary, to see there the proof of its weakness.*
>
> *A European King needs to obtain the support of the legislative body to fulfill the task that the constitution imposes on him, because this task is immense. A European constitutional King is not only the executor of the law; the care of its execution so completely devolves onto him that, if the law is against him, he would be able*

to paralyze its force. He needs the chambers to make the law; the chambers need him to execute it; they are two powers that cannot live without each other; the gears of government stop at the moment when there is discord between them.

In America, the President cannot stop the making of laws; he cannot escape the obligation to execute them. His zealous and sincere support is undoubtedly useful, but it is not necessary to the course of government. In everything essential that he does, he is directly or indirectly subject to the legislature; where he is entirely independent of it, he can hardly do anything. So it is his weakness, and not his strength, that allows him to live in opposition to the legislative power.

In Europe, there must be agreement between the King and the Chambers, because there can be a serious struggle between them. In America, agreement is not required, because the struggle is impossible.

Most presidential countries adopt principles that approximate the executive branch more to the constitutional king's powers that Tocqueville describes than to the American president's powers at the time of Tocqueville. This difference exists since the dawn of Latin American presidential republics: "in the typical Latin American republic high expectations rapidly developed that the new presidents would be 'elected kings with the name of presidents'—in Simón Bolívar's words— able to lead and secure the sovereignty of the newly created countries," as Colomer (2013) writes in his aptly named article, "Elected Kings with the Name of Presidents. On the Origins of Presidentialism in the United States and Latin America."

Tocqueville wrote about a different period of the history of the US. As Poguntke and Webb (2005) write, "US presidential history is clearly divided into two constitutional epochs, with FDR as the watershed (Pious, 1979; see also Fabbrini's chapter in this volume). In fact, its formal prerequisites notwithstanding, Woodrow Wilson (1885) would refer to the American government of his time as 'congressional government.' And one may conclude that American presidentialism only became truly presidentialized with the advent of the 'imperial presidency' of the post-FDR era (Lowi, 1985; Schlesinger, 1973)."

Even with these changes, Silva, Vieira, and Araujo (2017) show that many of the differences between America and other presidential countries persist to this day and that the American president has a weak capacity to control the cabinet in comparison to counterparts in other presidential democracies. Limongi (2006) in turn notes that the limited legislative capacity of the US president is the exception for presidential systems, not the rule. Thus, it is a mistake to think of the American system as the quintessential model of presidentialism. The US may be the original presidential country, but it is by no means typical.

Furthermore, to the extent that the American president does have independent power, parties still traditionally hold a lot of influence over his or her actions because the candidate selection process has been traditionally controlled by the two major parties (Cohen et al., 2009). It must be noted, however, that one of the just cited book's authors, Marty Cohen, believes that the pattern may be changing. In an interview with National Public Radio in 2016, he declared that "there's a real possibility that we're already into a different era [...] that probably began in 2004."[11]

Now that we understand the differences between the American presidential system and the systems observed in the majority of other countries that are called presidential, we may turn to Howell and Moe's thesis. As previously argued, a model is only as strong as its premises. Howell and Moe's (2016) premises about the behavior of presidents, however, are not realistic:

Crucial features set presidents apart from members of Congress. The first is that presidents are truly national leaders with national constituencies who think in national terms about national

---

[11]   *https://www.npr.org/2016/06/21/482357936/*
    celebrities-lies-and-outsiders-how-this-election-surprised-one-political-scienti

problems—and they are far less likely than legislators to become captive to narrow or local special-interest pressures. They are politicians. They are not perfect. Their policy agendas won't please everyone. But compared to members of Congress, they are paragons of national leadership.

Second, presidents occupy the highest office in the land, having reached the pinnacle not only of their careers but of their entire lives—and as a result, invariably, they are strongly motivated by concerns about their legacies. Their legacies, in turn, are ultimately defined—by historians, most notably—not on the basis of day-to-day public opinion or short-term events but rather on the basis of demonstrated success in crafting durable, effective policy solutions to important national problems. Members of Congress are not driven by such lofty concerns. They are famously myopic, incremental, and parochial; they think about the next election, and they use policies for short term and often local advantage.

Third, presidents are chief executives motivated and positioned to provide a coherent approach to the whole of government, whereas Congress can provide nothing of the sort. Its hundreds of members are mainly concerned about the various parts of government that matter to them as parochial politicians. Congress takes a piecemeal approach to the countless separate policies, programs, and agencies of government while presidents care about the entire corpus of government and about making it work.

For these reasons, presidents are wired to be the nation's problem-solvers in chief and to use the powers of their leadership to promote effective government.

If we look at the history of the US since independence, this account by Howell and Moe is not completely inaccurate. That would be a misleading guide, however. Former US presidents have never had the kind of power Howell and Moe propose. To determine what behavior should be expected from presidents with increased powers, we should study systems that do grant such powers—call it a "political Lucas critique." Lucas (1976) summarized his famous argument as such: "Given that the structure of an econometric model consists of optimal decision rules of economic agents, and that optimal decision rules vary systematically with changes in the structure of series relevant to the decision maker, it follows that any change in policy will systematically alter the structure of econometric models." The somewhat involved prose can better be clarified with an example from Harford (2015): "It turns out that saying, 'High inflation has always been correlated with low unemployment, so we can tackle unemployment by accepting higher inflation' is a bit like saying, 'Fort Knox has never been robbed, so we can save money by sacking the guards.' You can't look just at the empirical data, you need also to think about incentives." An examination of the behavior of presidents with great power, however, shows how dangerous they can be (Shugart and Carey, 1992).

Howell and Moe's description of the historical behavior of American presidents may not be completely inaccurate, but it still has issues. Their first point—presidents respond to a national constituency, congresspeople to local constituencies—is problematic because they assume *too much responsiveness* from members of Congress to their constituencies. When they say that politicians are "captive to narrow or local special-interest pressures," they implicitly assume that they will naturally behave that way because otherwise they will be voted out. Research on accountability, however, gives some nuance to this idea. As Achen and Bartels (2017) put it,

> The positions of elected officials are usually no more than mildly correlated with those of their constituents. Apparent disparities are persistent and sometimes substantial, notwithstanding the pressures toward congruence arising from electoral competition.

The second point also has problems. It may be true that presidents care about their legacies. But they are also subject to the same selfish motives as everyone else. With greater power, they have more opportunities to fulfill selfish motives. But even when they are concerned with their legacies and how history will view them, there are reasons to believe their incentives may not be well aligned with their people's. As Rossiter (1960) puts it, "A man cannot possibly be judged a great President unless he holds office in great times. [...] We have no right even to consider a [president great] unless he, too, presides over the nation in challenging years." (Nice, 1984). If presidents are "obsessed with gaining legacies as strong, successful leaders," as Moe and Howell argue, then we should be wary that they may be particularly prone to accept risks of crises, both internal and external, that other actors would not accept.

Finally, the third point still suffers from issues. While it may be true that the "hundreds of members [of Congress] are mainly concerned about the various parts of government that matter to them as parochial politicians" (Howell and Moe, 2016), it is not true that the weighting of these interests through majority voting is incapable of forming a coherent policy. Indeed, the very notion of democracy presupposes that people who do not necessarily "care about the entire corpus of government and about making it work"—as the authors say—can still make government work. Fortunately, this optimistic view of democracy is true under some conditions, which will be discussed below (see the chapter on Arrow's paradox). Still, an argument that self-interested voters are incapable of making decisions that ultimately benefit not just their constituency but the whole country is an argument for an enlightened despot, not for a presidential democracy.

The idea that "presidents are chief executives motivated and positioned to provide a coherent approach to the whole of government," on the other hand, is too optimistic. Presidents are people, and they suffer from the same cognitive biases and are prone to personal preferences, as everyone else, so they are often neither willing nor able to provide a coherent approach to the whole of government.

It is probably because of such characteristics that Howell and Moe say that, if they deemed it feasible, a parliamentary system would be preferable.

Table 1.1 American and Brazilian presidential powers: Some key differences

Powers	Brazil	USA
Senior cabinet positions	Free choice, hiring, and firing	• Hiring depends on Senate confirmation. • Dismissal is settled as a presidential prerogative since 1926
Veto powers	Line-item veto	Veto only in entirety
Legislative powers	Most matters that are subject to regular laws (with some exceptions, such as nationality) but with limited duration	• No constitutionally predicted legislative powers. • Executive orders have increased in scope recently, however.
Budget powers	• President has exclusive power to introduce budget legislation • Constitutional limits to congressional modifications to budget proposals • Lack of agreement with Congress favors executive	Congress has "power of the purse"
Leaderships of state-owned enterprises (SOEs)	Freely appointed by the president or appointed by freely appointed subordinates of the president	Confirmation by the Senate

1.1.2 Formal theory

In sum, there is a virtual consensus in favor of parliamentarism among informal theorists. What do formal models say? There seems to be fewer models than the importance of the issue would justify. This is mostly due to how hard they are to develop, as Myerson (1999) notes. To talk about the theory, we will examine the one formal model that points to benefits of having dual legitimacy systems by Persson, Roland, and Tabellini (1997, henceforth PRT). *For each of the assumptions that are violated, we have reasons to conclude that parliamentary systems are superior.* In this sense, what PRT show are the stringent conditions necessary for us to believe presidential systems could possibly outperform parliamentary systems. In examining these formal models, I do not assess their logical validity (which I deem sound) but only their assumptions. Below is the list of assumptions which will be examined:

- Indefinite reelection for the executive

- Proper checks and balances

- Equal ability in politicians

- Rational self-interested voters

- Identical voters

1 Indefinite reelection for the executive

The relaxation of the first assumption would already undermine the benefits of separation of powers, according to the authors' own model. Since politicians are assumed to be self-interested, an executive who knows he will not be reappointed will simply take as much for himself as possible at the expense of the voters. However, most presidential countries do have limits on reelection. This is because there is a wide perception, according to Carey (2003), "as old as presidentialism itself" that indefinite reelection represents a risk for democracy survival, as presidents tend to be reelected frequently by the sheer power of the office (Glaeser 1997), and subsequent reelections would only concentrate more power at the hands of one person. According to Cheibub (2007), only 18% of pure presidential systems between 1946 and 1996 had no restrictions for reelection.

Parliamentary democracies, on the other hand, rarely have term limits. Even heads of government may stay in office for several years and not be considered a threat to democracy and power-sharing. This is the "rigidity" issue of presidential systems that Linz (1994) talks about, as seen above.

2 Proper checks and balances

The second assumption does not seem to apply for the clear majority of presidential democracies. PRT determine that checks and balances require two conditions: "(i) there is a conflict of interests between the executive and the legislature; (ii) legislative decision-making requires joint agreement by both bodies." They show that if "the latter condition is [not] met, separation of powers makes voters worse off by creating a common-pool problem." So if this condition is violated, then separation of powers could end up being detrimental, as models by Brennan and Hamlin (1994) and Diermeier and Myerson (1995) show. However, the history of presidential countries shows that it is very often the case that one power can act without the support of the other. Indeed, the very idea of the separation of powers presupposes independent action. By PRT's definition of separation, it seems that different chambers of the legislature would be considered separate powers, which is not the case.[12]

3 Equal ability in politicians

PRT also assume that making good policy is not an issue for politicians—they can all deliver benefits to the population if they so wish. Buisseret (2016) introduces the possibility of there being some high- and low-ability politicians, a condition that voters cannot always directly perceive. In this case, the separation of powers would not be optimal from the voter's point of view.

---

[12] The reader may sense a possible contradiction with Tocqueville's premise that a requirement of agreement would be detrimental for a country, while the "proper checks and balances" premise concludes that a requirement of agreement is good. The contradiction, however, only serves to further demonstrate the difficult conditions necessary for presidentialism to be better. If the separate powers are required to act together, paralysis and conflict may ensue, for reasons mentioned by Tocqueville but not contemplated in PRT's model. If they are free to act independently, then separation of powers does worse because of reasons that are contemplated in PRT's model. Remember that Tocqueville did not presume the president could act independently of Congress. He presumed the president was not decisive for the actions of American government. The true situation seems to be that presidential systems need enough agreement to provoke crisis of inaction but also to allow for sufficient independence such that one branch may interfere with the other—a "worse of both worlds" scenario.

The intuition behind Buisseret's (2016) model is as follows. Suppose there are high- and low-ability politicians. Every policy must have a proposer and a veto player (who can endorse or reject the proposal). Voters have a limited capacity of evaluating the consequences of policies—they can only evaluate the quality of a policy if it does get implemented. If a veto player has low ability, then he or she will not be able to adequately assess the quality of the proposal. If they never veto anything, then voters will realize he or she is a low-ability politician and will substitute them. Since these low-ability politicians want to keep their positions, they will veto potentially good policies just to show they are doing something.

This is not merely a theoretical concern. As Pinker (2018) puts it, "[e]xperiments have shown that a critic who pans a book is perceived as more competent than a critic who praises it, and the same may be true of critics of society."

4   Rational self-interested voters

The rational self-interested voters assumption deserves a longer discussion. The assumption of rationality is widely used in most models but is strongly contested. The standard assumption is that voters rationally analyze the options at the voting booth and choose the candidates who are most likely to increase their personal well-being. But as Downs (1957) points out, a rational self-interested citizen would never vote. The probability that any single vote would affect the outcome is vanishingly small. Even if politicians do make decisions that will affect citizens' welfare in meaningful ways, the necessary effort involved in staying informed of what the issues are and what is the expected quality of different candidates would not compensate the low expected value of their single vote. The natural state for a voter would be of "rational ignorance," and voters would have no incentive to go to the polls.

Given that people do vote, in large numbers, there is a puzzle to be explained. Brennan and Buchanan (1984) offer the explanation of "expressive voting"—further developed in Brennan and Lomasky (1993) and in Hamlin and Jennings (2011). Casting a vote would be like rooting for a team, where "neither the act of voting nor the direction of a vote cast can be explained as a means to achieving a particular political outcome, any more than spectators attend a game as a means of securing the victory for their team" (Brennan and Buchanan, 1984). According to this explanation, people will not vote for their preferred policies and the candidates more likely to pursue them but will instead privilege how their vote will make them be perceived by their peers or how they will view themselves.

Concerned that the expressive voting model would imply an implausible amount of hypocrisy on the part of the voters, Caplan (2007) suggests a modification, proposing instead the idea of "rational irrationality." Voters have certain genuine preferences for policies that, if implemented, would leave them worse off. If they were to be decisive on such issues, then they would have the incentives to become better informed, confront those preferences, and make the most rational decision. However, given that their chances of being decisive are so small, they may indulge in their harmful preferences without direct consequences from their votes. The result is that policies end up reflecting these irrational preferences instead of the rational preferences voters would express if they had reason to believe their votes would impact the outcomes.

In favor of the rationality of voting, Edlin, Gelman, and Kaplan (2007) argue that while it is true that from a purely self-interested viewpoint, the benefits of voting do not compensate the efforts, if we admit that voters care about the fate of their fellow citizens, it may make perfect sense to participate in elections. According to their calculations, in the US, the expected value of a single vote, on average, can be US$30,000 or higher.[13] So even if the rational self-interested voter hypothesis is no longer plausible, the jury would still be out on a rational, altruistic voter. The latter hypothesis will depend on how much value voters place, on average, on the well-being of their fellow citizens, how much it costs them to get informed, how much value they assign of feeling and looking good, and how attached they are to their irrational preferences.

---

[13]   Because of the electoral college system in the US, a vote can be more or less decisive—which means more or less valuable—depending on whether or not it is cast in a swing state.

Given Edlin, Gelman, and Kaplan's argument, the issue of voter rationality becomes an empirical one. There are two types of rationality worth considering—strict rationality and common sense rationality. In the rational choice tradition, "rationality" requires only that voters have transitive preferences—meaning that if they prefer A to B and B to C, they also prefer A to C—and preferences are comparable (i.e., for any choice, a rational agent will be able to say whether she prefers one or the other or if she is indifferent). In common parlance, we might deem people irrational if we believe their preferences are absurd (e.g., if they treat trash as collectible items) or if they have manifestly wrong beliefs about how to achieve their preferences (e.g., if they destroy company property in the hopes of getting a promotion). Both types of rationality are important for evaluating the quality of institutions. Even if voters might be rational in a strict sense (something that is really hard to disprove), if they are more prone to act according to demonstrably wrong beliefs in one system than in another, then a case can be made in favor of the system that delivers more rational policies in the common sense of the word.

The general undesirability of having policies based in demonstrably wrong beliefs is the argument that supports the empirical analysis in Caplan's (2007) *Myth of the Rational Voter: Why Democracies Choose Bad Policies*. Voters have several biases that are deemed wrong when compared to the benchmark of experts' opinions. These biases are categorized as anti-market, anti-foreign, make-work ("a tendency to underestimate the economic benefits from conserving labor" Caplan, 2007), and pessimistic. Caplan provides various statistics and examples of situations where the biases may be observed. His arguments resonate even among principled critics of his thesis. In a review, journalist Chris Hayes[14] writes that "you must confront the fact that voters can often be stunningly under-informed and that majoritarianism run amok can lead to persecution, hatred and injustice. Reading Caplan's book, then, is both bracing and necessary because it forces the reader to stare into the abyss."

Hayes, however, believes that the academic consensus is that voters are rational. Dowding (2005, p. 442) shows quite clearly this is not so:

---

[14]   *https://chrishayes.org/articles/whos-afraid-democracy/.*

We know why people vote, or at least we know why people think they vote, because in surveys they have told us. The problem for rational choice theory is that the answer is boring, and it is not clear that it makes people instrumentally rational [...]

In fact, models of expressive voting (Brennan and Lomasky, 1993; Schuessler, 2000, 2001) do produce predictions that are consistent with empirical evidence. The marginal considerations we saw above still operate with an expressive component. The expressive component could not be the whole story or voters should not be too upset if it turns out the ballot box where they cast their vote was compromised so their vote was not counted. But voters do get upset, which suggests expressing yourself is not the only factor, especially since many people want to keep their actual vote secret. Furthermore, if all one wanted was to express a preference then there would be no room for tactical voting and there is evidence that some vote strategically (Cox, 1997; Franklin, Niemi, and Whitten, 1994).

Nevertheless the 'D' answer [N: the expressive voting answer], despite being simple, despite being empirically verified by stated preference evidence, consistent with aggregate data evidence, and, if not properly tested, corroborated by Barry's and Knack's evidence, does not find much favour among political scientists whether rational choice advocates or critics. Why? Because they want deeper reasons.

Dowding demonstrates that the resistance of rational choice is more due to theorists wanting it to be right than to how well it fits the evidence. In this sense, there is less of an academic consensus over what the evidence says than a presumption, contrary to the evidence, about how voters should behave. One should also note that while a "pure hypocrisy" interpretation of the expressive voting theory has the limitations mentioned by Dowding (voters do get sincerely upset; they do vote tactically), an interpretation that incorporates Caplan's rational irrationality hypothesis is perfectly consistent.

Given how far public opinion stands from the ideal policies Caplan (2007, p. 158) envisions, he himself is puzzled:

> *Before studying public opinion, many wonder why democracy does not work better. After one becomes familiar with the public's systematic biases, however, one is struck by the opposite question: Why does democracy work as well as it does? How do the unpopular policies that sustain the prosperity of the West survive? Selective participation is probably one significant part of the answer. It is easy to criticize the beliefs of the median voter, but at least he is less deluded than the median nonvoter.*

Selective participation cannot be the main driver of the difference between public opinion and the quality of policies, however. Even the median voter, more informed than the median non-voter, has beliefs that are far removed from economic consensus and existing policies. Brennan and Hamlin's (2000) hypothesis is that, while expressive voting selects bad policies, the representatives chosen by the people are high quality, with more integrity and competence than the average citizen. Is this true? Most people would find the hypothesis absurd. Approval of Congress in the US is traditionally low and currently stands at 18% (Gallup, 2019), but evidence discussed below suggests that people do send some of their best and brightest to Congress.

Naturally, there are numerous scandals stemming from Congress, and comedians rejoice at blunders that make congresspeople seem to not be the sharpest tool in the shed. But we must bear in mind the level of scrutiny that these people endure, the level of power they have (which makes deviating from public interest more tempting), and the number of interests they must attend to at the same time[15] (which might be behind

---

[15] Recall that, when dealing with Howell and Moe's thesis in Section 1.1.1 (Informal theory), I said that those authors assume too much responsiveness from members of Congress to their constituencies. There is no contradiction why my statement above that members of Congress need to attend to many interests at the same time. First, the fact that they may not be as responsive to constituents in their voting behavior does not mean they are willing to alienate voters with controversial

some of the less-inspired declarations). The proper question is how the average citizen would behave if they had so much power. Some people believe that they would fare much better because many democracies would in fact be better described as kakistocracies—or "government by the worst." Their argument is that the kind of ambition necessary to be elected would ensure that only the least virtuous ever reach power.

That argument, however, exaggerates on the pessimism regarding voters' capacities to select good politicians. Even if the worst politicians have every incentive to try to get to power, voters may prevent them from doing so. There is no contradiction in affirming voters' incompetence in evaluating policies and insisting on their skill in evaluating people. Once we think of the question in evolutionary terms, the puzzle disappears. Being a good judge of character—of people who are reliable and smart enough to be good cooperators—is an essential survival trait for a person. People accurately judge personality (Naumann et al., 2009), even in environments with very low background information (e.g., just by looking at pictures or observing regular conversation). As acquaintance with a person grows, so does the accuracy of his or her judgment of that person. Notably, the capacity to judge conscientiousness, arguably the most relevant personality trait with respect to the integrity of a potential member of Congress, increases rapidly after little acquaintance (Lee and Ashton, 2017).

Voter capacity to select politicians with desirable characteristics is confirmed by evidence. Dal Bó et al. (2017) look at municipal data from Sweden to assess the quality of Swedish representatives. They find the following:

> First, politicians are on average significantly smarter and better leaders than the population they represent. Second, this positive selection is present even when conditioning on family (and hence

---

statements. Second, even if they are not as accountable to voters as one would think at first, they are still accountable to other members of Congress. The importance of negotiation within members of Congress will be made clearer in the next item, with the discussion of Parisi's (2003) model.

social) background, suggesting that individual competence is key for selection. Third, the representation of social background, whether measured by parental earnings or occupational social class, is remarkably even. Fourth, there is at best a weak trade-off in selection between competence and social representation, mainly due to strong positive selection of politicians of low (parental) socioeconomic status. A broad implication of these facts is that it is possible for democracy to generate competent and socially representative leadership.

One objection to Dal Bó et al.'s (2017) argument for voter competence in other settings may be that Swedish members of parliament have a generally good reputation and have the trust of around 70% of their constituents (OECD, 2017). But while in the US trust is much lower (Gallup, 2018), we still find evidence that elected politicians are extremely well qualified according to usual standards.

Educational achievement is the one of the best proxies for job performance. As Dal Bó et al. (2017) explain, "absent direct data on the underlying intelligence or personality of politicians, the existing empirical literature has relied on education or pre-office income (Bäck and Öhrvall, 2004; Dal Bó, Dal Bó, and Snyder, 2009; Ferraz and Finan, 2009; Merlo et al., 2010; Galasso and Nannicini, 2011; Besley and Reynal-Querol, 2011; Gagliarducci and Paserman, 2012)." Education is a reasonable choice because it is what employers in all sectors—private, governmental, and non-governmental—rely upon the most to select employees they will trust to handle their business deals, property, and sensitive information. There is also evidence that education is related to ability and integrity (De Vries, de Vries, and Born, 2011).

Members of the US Congress are remarkably well educated. Geiger, Bialik, and Gramlich (2019) write the following:

Nearly all members of Congress now have college degrees. In the 115th Congress, 95% of House members and 100% of senators have received a four-year degree or higher. In the 79th Congress (1945–1947), by comparison, 56% of House members and 75% of senators had degrees. The share of representatives and senators with college degrees has steadily increased over time. The educational attainment of Congress members far outpaces that of the overall US population. In 2015, just 33% of American adults ages 25 and older said they had completed a bachelor's degree or more, according to the US Census Bureau.

Members of Congress are far above average, not only by the share of them with college degrees but also the prestige of their alma mater. Michel Nietzel[16] writes

The collegiate pedigrees of this freshman class are impressive. Consider just the 30 highest ranked institutions on the Forbes 2018 Top Colleges list. 40 of the 102 new Senators and Representatives received at least one of their degrees from a college on that list. Add in other highly regarded schools like Carnegie Mellon, Wesleyan, Colgate, the Naval Academy, Kenyon, and the universities of Virginia, Minnesota and Wisconsin, and more than half of the group earned an undergraduate or graduate degree from one of the nation's most esteemed colleges. The group features three Rhodes Scholars: New Jersey's Andy Kim (also recognized as a Truman Scholar), Tom Malinowski (New Jersey) who earned a Master's degree from Oxford in 1991 and New York's Antonio Delgado, who in addition to receiving a Master's from Oxford, can boast of playing on the last Colgate basketball team to make the NCAA tourney.

5   Identical voters

After a long discussion of voter rationality, we turn to the last assumption in PRT's model. Identical voters are perhaps the most extreme assumption. People do not have the same preferences by a long shot. Indeed, by positing identical voters, the model becomes equivalent to a regular

---

[16]   https://www.forbes.com/sites/michaeltnietzel/2018/12/10/
the-college-profile-of-the-116th-congresss-first-year-class/#4ea33f173bcc

principal-agent model since identical voters would all have the same opinion and could therefore be substituted by just one person.

The fact that people do not have the same preferences is extremely consequential. If there were a reliable way to give every person a vote and to elicit a socially optimal decision, then introducing voters with different preferences would only unnecessarily complicate the model. But Arrow's impossibility theorem demonstrates that this is not the case. Unfortunately, there is no easy way to explain the results of the theorem. I will then only say that under some reasonable assumptions about preferences, the theorem shows that voting procedures may reach radically different results, and these results are unstable, which means that for every new election, there can be a different outcome. What many political scientists do to circumvent this problem is to propose that voter preferences fall along only one dimension (we may think of this as how "leftist" or how "rightist" a person is). However, this is a far-fetched proposal. Not only does it imply a strong correlation between someone's opinion on abortion, taxes, and war, but it also implies equal preferences on distributive matters – and by "equal preferences on distributive matters" I am not talking about preferences over how equal or unequal a society may be on the aggregate level, I mean that people would have to assign as much value to getting more money themselves as they assign to their neighbor, or that elected politicians would give equal priority to campaign allies and rivals when choosing members of their governmentAs Boncheck and Shepsle (1996) write, "sharing out benefits and burdens, or what is known as 'distributive politics' is inherently cyclical in majoritarian settings." Given that all politics involve sharing benefits and burdens, even if we may strive for that to be minimized, it follows that we may always expect voting cycles in purely majoritarian settings as the number of issues and voters grows.

Assemblies solve the problems that Arrow's theorem points to. A crucial implicit assumption by Arrow is that there are no enforceable transactions between voters. Indeed, if voters can communicate, transact, and commit to their transactions, then Coase's theorem applies, as demonstrated by Parisi (2003). Coase's theorem proves that if transactions costs are low enough, then parties making transactions can achieve the socially optimal decision.

How does this work? We will not get into the mathematics, only the intuition. Suppose there are three voters, A, B, and C, who must divide $300 among them. Suppose also that they have diminishing marginal return to money (i.e., they value going from $1 to $2 more than they value going from $200 to $201). We are using the majority voting criteria, so two votes get to decide.

Suppose that any of the possible ways to share the $300 is allowed—$100 for A, B, and C; $300 for A and nothing for B and C, etc. Suppose further that they can talk about how they will vote, but after the votes are cast, the money is divided by exactly how it was voted. One party may make a promise, but since contracts are not enforceable and in our model we are imagining that they are purely selfish, it is assumed that they would not fulfill the promise (I will talk about the effects of relaxing such an unrealistic assumption about how selfish people are below).

In that case, two of them will vote together to divide all of the $300 between them and will leave nothing to the third one. How exactly how they will divide the $300 is uncertain. Any result, such as $150A/$150B/$0C, $0A/$290B/$10C—is equally likely from the specifications—but any combination that includes money for all three of them will lose to one that excludes one of them. To see this, consider the most intuitive solution, $100 for each. A may propose to B that, instead of gaining only $100, they can each get $150. Now C makes a counterproposal: B will get $200, and C is content with only the $100 that they would originally get. A, who first proposed to deviate from the equal division, is now desperate and makes another proposal: B may keep $290, and A will be happy with only $10. C, seeing that it does not make sense to give A such privilege, proposes instead to B that they each get $150. You see where this is going. There is no stable solution, but since one only needs two votes to decide, none of the solutions involve sharing money among the three.

What Parisi (2003) shows is that, if you allow transactions to happen freely and are able to make agreements enforceable, you will reach the best decision—the one that maximizes utility given their preferences—which is to divide the money equally.

This relates directly to the differences between presidential and parliamentary systems. Individual voters in the general population cannot conduct these kinds of collective transactions. Even if it is true (and it is) that people are not as selfish as the model implies,[17] as the number of participants increases, the uncertainty of cooperation also goes up and selfish motivations dominate. Parliament members, however, can engage in such transactions and do (in fact, they are commonly accused of doing this). Their constant interaction ensures that those who do not stand by their word will not be forgotten and properly punished. Even if transaction costs are high, limiting the ability of achieving Coasean benefits, the fact that parliament members vote issue-by-issue, instead of the necessary bundling of issues involved in choosing just one president, means parliaments can still reach an optimal solution (Luppi and Parisi, 2012). Parties, which are able to enforce discipline in their representatives (but could never have that kind of power over their voters) also may help reduce transaction costs. As Ostrom (2009) writes, "the impact of group size on the transaction costs of self-organizing tends to be negative given the higher costs of getting users together and agreeing on changes." Or as Wittman (1995) says, "the small size of Congress reduces transaction costs, thereby allowing Pareto-improving trades and bargains. An inefficient method of transferring wealth from one district to another can be defeated by an efficient transfer."

The common argument is that presidents represent "the will of the people," while members of parliaments, even though also elected, represent particular interests. This line of thought gets it exactly backward. By being able to transact votes, parliaments may approximate the socially optimal outcome, whereas presidents will represent any of the numerous agendas that could conceivably win the election when a society is trapped by Arrow's paradox.

---

[17] Indeed, leading evolutionary theories about morality sustain that the reason people are not that selfish is to better take advantage of situations such as the one described above. See Greene (2013).

1.2 The evidence

This section looks at the evidence in three types of organizations to support the hypothesis that parliamentary systems are better. I naturally rely on the evidence from national governments but also use auxiliary evidence from corporations and local governments. Of course, these three types of organizations all differ in numerous ways, but all of the models discussed up until now (e.g., the PRT model or the Brennan model) could be equally applicable to all of them, irrespective of them being sovereign or not or whether or not they are a for-profit enterprise. I develop these ideas further below. In any instance, it is a task left for the critic to model how these differences would affect the outcome of development in important ways.

1.2.1 National governments

Stability. Linz (1994) is credited for the near consensus that arose in the 1990s that presidential systems are less stable than parliamentary ones. However, later empirical papers on the issue, discussed below, suggest some of that consensus has dissolved. Even though there are a variety of studies with different results, this does not imply that the null hypothesis of no effect should be favored. If the effects of parliamentary (compared to presidential) systems were mere random variation around zero, then effect sizes should be, on average, smaller than they are, and they should not be one-sided. This means we must dig into the studies and see which of them are right and which are wrong.

Przeworski et al. (2000, p. 136) provide the seminal work that finds greater stability in parliamentary systems—*Democracy and Development*. They use a relatively restrictive definition of democracy and find that parliamentary regimes are more stable, even after inserting a number of controls: "presidential democracies are simply more brittle under all economic and political conditions." Kapstein and Converse (2008) find the opposite result by adopting a definition of democracy that does not require, as in the Przeworski et al. (2000) study, a successful change in the party in power. The authors capture numerous democratic reversals in short-lived parliamentary systems, notably in Africa. Their study suggests that parliamentary systems are less stable in their first years and are more stable after a while.

Robinson and Torvik (2016) explain these short-lived parliamentary systems that Kapstein and Converse deal with. If leaders want to prolong their tenure in power and have greater chances of doing so in a presidential, rather than in a parliamentary, system, then there are more incentives for them to forsake parliamentary systems before they are mature enough to resist authoritarian urges than there are to abandon presidential ones. Thus, parliamentary systems are abandoned in their early years because they are correctly perceived by a prospective autocrat as being more conducive to sharing a broader range of power.

With respect to null findings, Cheibub (2007) writes the most cited work. According to Przeworski,[18] Cheibub's analysis "puts the controversy to rest." The author found that, when he controlled for military legacy (i.e., whether or not a country was under a military dictatorship instead of a different kind of authoritarian arrangement prior to democratization), the effects of parliamentarism disappeared. Evidence indicates that the judgment by Przeworski was hasty. There are reasons to believe Cheibub's results were spurious. As Cheibub (2007) himself puts it, he observed that before controlling for military legacy, "[w]hatever one controls for, a difference in the survival rates of parliamentary and presidential democracies is still there." The problem with controlling for an increasing number of variables is that at some point, you may find a spurious result.

Further evidence that this may be a spurious result is that Cheibub himself—when co-authoring the aforementioned *Democracy and Development* with Przeworski, Alvarez, and Limongi—finds, under different specifications, that military legacy cannot explain the greater instability of presidential systems:

---

[18]   On the back cover of Cheibub's book.

If presidentialism is a military legacy, then perhaps presidential democracies last for shorter periods simply because they emerge in countries where the military is politically relevant. We thus need to compare separately the hazard rates for parliamentary and presidential democracies distinguished by their origins. It is apparent that a military legacy shortens the life of democracy regardless of its institutional framework. Democracies that emerged from civilian dictatorships died at the rate of 0.0158, with an expected life of 63.4 year; those that succeeded military dictatorships died at the rate of 0.0573, with an expected life of 17.5 years. Parliamentary democracies, however, are still more stable regardless of their origins. *Given civilian origins, parliamentary democracies died at the rate of 0.0119 and had an expected life of 83.7 years, and presidential democracies died at the rate of 0,0329, with an expected life of 30.4 years. Given military origins, parliamentary systems died at the rate of 0.0400, with an expected life of 25 years, and presidential systems died at the rate of 0.0628 and had an expected life of 16 years. Thus, again, the stability of democracies seems to be an effect of their institutional frameworks, not only of their origins. [emphasis added]*

When other authors use different specifications to try to replicate the effect of military legacy, it disappears. The presidential effect on democratic breakdown, however, is seen once again. As Aydogan (2019) elaborates, if you do not restrict your observations to democracies but instead include anocracies, which are governments halfway between democracies and autocracies —that may be classified as presidential or parliamentary—then the effect reappears. This approach makes sense. Constitutional arrangements affect societies even if they are not entirely democratic. The Glorious Revolution is widely considered an example of a consequential constitutional arrangement, but at that time, voting for parliament was restricted to less than 10% of the adult male British population. Switzerland, which is universally considered a mature and stable democracy, only started allowing women to vote in the 1970s.

Today, anybody who believes that a country that does not allow women to vote is democratic would be dismissed from the debate on democracy.

In fact, the causality between parliamentary and presidential constitutions and greater democracy (as defined by Cheibub's standards) may then mean that having a constitution of a presidential or a parliamentary nature may affect how democratic you are. If this is true, then by restricting the sample to full democracies, Cheibub ends up introducing a "bad control," in the terms of Angrist and Pischke (2008). Bad controls are "variables that are themselves outcome variables in the notional experiment at hand." Here is how Angrist and Pischke (2008, p. 64) illustrate the problem:

> Suppose we are interested in the effects of a college degree on earnings and that people can work in one of two occupations, white collar and blue collar. A college degree clearly opens the door to higher-paying white collar jobs. Should occupation therefore be seen as an omitted variable in a regression of wages on schooling? After all, occupation is highly correlated with both education and pay. Perhaps it is best to look at the effect of college on wages for those within an occupation, say white collar only. The problem with this argument is that once we acknowledge the fact that college affects occupation, comparisons of wages by college degree status within an occupation are no longer apples-to-apples, even if college degree completion is randomly assigned.

The underlying theme by Cheibub (2007) can be paraphrased as it does not matter if you have a presidential or parliamentary system; if you have a democracy, your chances of experiencing a coup are about the same[19]. My point is that this could be replied with "well, your chances

---

[19] Some readers of earlier versions of this text pushed back against this characterization of Cheibub's (2007) overall thesis, so I feel a need to include quotes to support it: "the reason for the instability of presidential democracies lies not in any intrinsic features of presidentialism but rather in the conditions under which they emerge – namely, the fact that presidential regimes tend to exist in countries that are also more likely to suffer from dictatorships led by the

of ever becoming a full democracy are much better under a parliamentary constitution." Indeed, Teorell and Lindberg (2019), examining a new dataset that covers the period 1789–2016, find that

> *[E]lections, to the extent they are at all held, are generally less free and fair when executives are appointed through military force. Less self-evident, however, is that elections under directly elected executives are about as marred by fraud when hereditary succession dominates as when executives are elected according to the ruling-party mechanism. (...) The only elections that really stand out in terms of freedom and fairness are the ones held under an executive subject to the confidence requirement.*

When Aydogan (2019) analyzes how prone presidential versus parliamentary regimes are to coups, he includes countries that would not be classified as democracies by Cheibub. This change in approach once again reveals that presidential systems are indeed more likely to experience interruptions. Likewise, Sing (2010) cannot replicate Cheibub's finding that military legacy could explain the difference in the survival rate of parliamentary versus presidential democracies.

CHEIBUB'S PROBLEMATIC REFUTATION OF LINZIAN MECHANISMS FOR DEMOCRATIC BREAKDOWN IN PRESIDENTIAL DEMOCRACIES

Perhaps we have reason to believe that presidential regimes indeed are more unstable than parliamentary ones. But this does not necessarily reinstate Linz's views. Did Cheibub not show that Linzian mechanisms failed? Unfortunately for Cheibub, the supposed refutation of Linz's theory is problematic. Cheibub portrays Linz's thesis as dependent on a complete lack of incentives for coalition formation in presidential systems and the prevalence of minority governments: "Recall that at the root of the view that

---

military"; "From a strictly institutional point of view, presidentialism can be as stable as parliamentarism"; "presidential institutions do not cause the instability of presidential democracies".

presidentialism causes democratic instability is the idea that presidential institutions—owing to the independence of the executive and the legislative branches—provide no incentive for coalition formation" (Cheibub, 2007). The author provided a flowchart that is meant to summarize Linz's thesis:

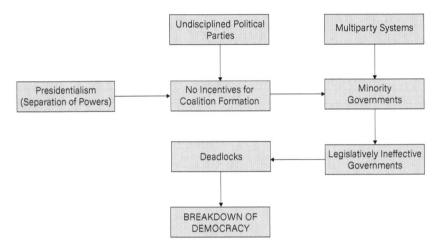

Figure 1.1 How Cheibub (2007) interprets Linz's thesis

But the lack of incentives for coalition building is but one of the issues that Linz identifies as problematic for presidential systems. If we recall Lijphart's summary above (Section 1.1.1), Linz identifies four major problems with presidential democracies:

- dual democratic legitimacy
- rigidity
- winner take all
- politics of personality

The incentives for coalition formation and the prevalence of minority governments are part of only one of the major problems, the winner takes all issue. Cheibub never addresses the problem of dual democratic legitimacy. In Linz's (1994) words,

Under such circumstances, who, on the basis of democratic principles, is better legitimated to speak in the name of the people: the president, or the congressional majority that opposes his policies? Since both derive their power from the vote of the people in a free competition among well-defined alternatives, a conflict is always latent and sometimes likely to erupt dramatically; there is no democratic principle to resolve it, and the mechanisms that might exist in the constitution are generally complex, highly technical, legalistic, and, therefore, of doubtful democratic legitimacy for the electorate.

Neither does Cheibub deal with the tendency for personalization of politics in presidential regimes. He assumes that the president party's preferences perfectly align with the president's own preferences, which is certainly not true. Linz (1994), in turn, writes the following:

The personalized character of a presidential election makes possible, especially in the absence of a strong party system, the access to power of 'outsiders.' We mean by this candidates not identified with or supported by any political party, sometimes without any governmental or even political experience, on the basis of a populist appeal often based on hostility to parties and to parties and 'politicians.' The candidacy of such leaders might appear suddenly and capitalize on the frustrations of voters and their hopes for a 'savior.'

Even Cheibub's treatment of coalitions, the one argument against presidentialism with which he engages, is problematic. First, he reads too much from the Linzian literature with respect to coalition formation in presidential systems. As Cheibub himself writes,

"[presidential systems, a]cording to Mainwaring and Scully (195:33), [...] 'lack the institutionalized mechanisms of coalition building that exist in parliamentary democracy.' For Linz and Stepan (1996:181), 'parliamentarism over time develops many incentives

to produce coalitional majorities' whereas 'presidentialism has far fewer coalition-inducing incentives.' For Valenzuela (2004:16), 'parliamentary regimes are based on a political logic that urges cooperation and consensus within the context of coherent policies' yet 'the underlying logic of presidentialism is far more conflict-prone'" (emphasis added).

What these authors are saying, clearly, is that the incentives for coalition formation are fewer in parliamentary systems than in presidential systems. For Cheibub, however, this becomes, as previously cited, "presidential institutions—owing to the independence of the executive and the legislative branches—provide *no incentive* for coalition formation (Cheibub, 2007, emphasis added).

Cheibub does find that coalitions are less frequent in presidential countries, but he argues that they should be much rarer according to Linz. Maybe Linz did underestimate the capacity of presidents to build coalitions. But this in no way invalidates his whole thesis.

Development outcomes. The perils of presidentialism are not restricted to political stability; they appear on a range of development outcomes, which can be seen in the empirical literature. Empirical study of development outcomes started being produced only relatively recently. We have been talking about correlations between parliamentary systems and good development outcomes, but as is now common knowledge, correlation is not causation. The empirical studies mentioned in this section use a variety of techniques to try to estimate what could be causal effects. None of them are simple correlations between form of government and the outcome of interest. Two reasons stand out for this puzzling lapse. First, only recently statistical techniques were developed that could plausibly separate the various confounding effects involved with parliamentary systems and development. Second, there was a lack of data; however, we now have higher quality data for government forms and for economic performance.

Persson and Tabellini are considered the pioneers for the study of the economic consequences of systems of government, with their 2005 *The*

Economic Effects of Constitutions. The most reported result from this book appears to be the propensity for lower government spending in presidential systems. It is not clear, however, if this is good or bad in itself. More clearly supportive of the parliamentary hypothesis, they find that parliamentary systems have higher productivity, but the result is only significant at the 10% level, above the 5% standard. Contrary to our hypothesis, they find more graft in parliamentary systems (based on the Corruptions Perceptions Index). However, when they test the effect of system of government on an index of anti-diversion policies, which includes corruption, they find that parliamentary countries are better at preventing anti-diversion policies.

Persson and Tabellini's (2005) investigation of productivity was based on a cross-section sample. When Blume et al. (2009) replicated with an extended dataset, the result was not significant even at the 10% level—although the direction was still the same.[20] Gerring, Thacker, and Moreno (2009) examine 14 outcome measures in three policy areas: political development, economic development, and human development with panel data. This allows them to significantly expand on the number of observations compared to Persson and Tabellini. They are still unable to use a fixed effects approach, however, because of little variance in each country. Gerring, Thacker, and Moreno's (2009) strategy, then, is to introduce control variables to try to isolate the effect of government system. They find significant differences in favor of parliamentarism in 10 of the 14 outcome measures, with presidential systems not superior in any of them. Namely, parliamentary systems are associated with higher GDP per capita, better corruption control (in one of two measures examined but not the other), bureaucratic quality, rule of law, telephone mainlines, import duties, trade openness, investment rating, infant mortality, and literacy.

Knutsen (2011) in turn uses a fixed effects approach and finds significant benefits for growth in parliamentary systems for the period 1979–2002. He does not find, however, benefits in previous periods of his data, and when looking at the total sample (1899–2002), the results

---

[20] While non-significant findings tend to be disregarded in the academic literature, particularly if they fail even the 10% threshold, a Bayesian analysis uses all available evidence without assigning arbitrary thresholds. This will be clearer in Chapter 5.

are also insignificant. Binder (2018) finds there is less political pressure on central banks; Andersen and Aslaken (2008) find parliamentary countries are not subject to the natural resource curse; Martinez (2018) finds that growth statistics of parliamentary countries are more reliable, while presidential countries overestimate their growth rate (which means the growth difference may be even larger); Bartolini and Santolini (2017) find higher government effectiveness and regulatory quality in parliamentary systems; and Kohlscheen (2009) and Saiegh (2018) find that parliamentary countries have fewer debt crises.

McManus and Ozkan (2018) find that parliamentary systems grow faster than presidential systems and have less inflation and less inequality. In a follow-up article for a wide readership, the authors summarize their findings[21]:

> By using data from 119 countries across the period 1950 to 2015 and examining an extensive set of macroeconomic data, we find that parliamentary regimes are consistently better for a country's economy. On average, annual output growth is up to 1.2 percentage points higher, inflation is less volatile and 6 percentage points lower, and income inequality is up to 20% lower in countries governed by parliamentary systems. [...] When we categorize countries according to growth and income inequality, we find that 91% of the best performers—with above average growth and below average income inequality—are parliamentary regimes. In isolating the impact of the two forms of government, we consider a large set of other factors that are likely to influence economic performance such as geography, the legacy of colonial rule, religion and how long the country has been a democracy for.

McManus and Ozkan's work shows that, as forms of government are concerned, there is no trade-off between equality and efficiency;

---

[21] https://theconversation.com/
parliamentary-systems-do-better-economically-than-presidential-ones-111468

parliamentary systems dominate presidential ones and promote more of both goals of democracies.

In sum, despite not being unanimous, the state of the evidence points to a clear advantage of parliamentary systems. But these studies are all examining many of the same years and basically the same countries. If there are endogeneity issues that have not been accounted for in the studies' design, they may all be biased in the same direction. Therefore, we must look into evidence from other sources to increase confidence.

1.2.2 Corporations

Gregory: Is there any other point to which you
would wish to draw my attention?
Holmes: To the curious incident of the dog in the night-time.
Gregory: The dog did nothing in the night-time.
Holmes: That was the curious incident.
(Doyle, 2018)

At first glance, the organization of private businesses seem to offer the least amount of evidence for our purposes, for two reasons: 1) this would amount to an apples-to-oranges comparison of organizations with very different structures and histories, and 2) there is a lack of variation. The first reason is incorrect. The histories of corporate governance and governmental institutions are deeply intertwined, as can be seen in Freeman, Pearson, and Taylor's (2012, hereafter FPT) book or in Maier's (1993) paper. Public and corporate governance are not similar in name only; they attempt to solve large cooperation and coordination problems among large populations. As FPT show, corporate governance evolved in a very parallel manner to government: "The pervasiveness of political metaphors in the pamphlet literature and procedural records of joint-stock companies is evidence that these balances were viewed in political terms, reflecting the reshaping of the governmental land-scape—national and local—in the same period." Maier (1993) writes, "For contemporaries, the proliferation of corporations could signal, in effect,

an extension of American federalism down into day-to-day, local asso-
ciational relationships, so that 'the whole political system' was 'made
up of a concatenation of various corporations, political, civil, religions,
social and economical,' in which the nation itself was a 'great corporation, comprehending all others.'" The analogy between governments
and corporations is the basis for "Corporate governance: separation of
powers and checks and balances in Israeli corporate law," by Lurie and
Frenkel (2003).

In effect, the separation of state and business was blurred for many
years. Any function of a business can be performed by the state (and in
socialist countries, they are). Likewise, businesses have engaged in several activities that we deem to be the function of the state—not only the
more obvious such as health, education, and public transportation but
also the ones that we deem to be natural arenas for states, such as security (the University of Chicago, for example, has a department with full
police powers[22]), national defense (Kinsey, 2006), and even the textbook
example of a public good: lighthouses (Coase, 1974). When corporations
began operating, in fact, they were required to perform a public function.
As Maier (1993) writes, even in the 19th century, the "American Treatise
on the Law of Private Corporations Aggregate (1832) by Joseph K. Angell
and Samuel Ames continued to describe 'the successful promotion of
some design of public utility' as the purpose of corporations."

Further evidence of this close intertwinement comes from the rules
used in meetings in all sorts of organizations—churches, clubs, companies, unions. When these entities have to make decisions in the name of
the collective, they must follow the rules of "parliamentary procedure."
This name is not a coincidence. The most widely used manual for parliamentary procedure in the US is called Robert's Rules of Order and
was written after the author "became convinced of the need for a new
kind of parliamentary manual, *'based, in its general principles, upon the
rules and practices of Congress, and adapted, in its details, to the use of
ordinary societies'*" Robert et al. (2011; italics in the original).

---

[22] *https://www.chicagomaroon.com/2012/05/25/a-brief-history-of-the-ucpd/*

Companies constitutional agreements, or bylaws as they are usually called, have to deal with the same issues that Lijphart (1994) identifies as the defining characteristics of parliamentary versus presidential governments: whether the officers are directly elected by the members or are elected by the board, whether the officers are freely removed by the board, or whether executive decision-making depends on a collective or on an individual.

Having established corporations are indeed comparable to governments, we may turn to the second reason one might object to their being used as evidence for the benefits of parliamentary systems: a lack of variation in governance arrangements. Companies organized as presidential systems do not seem to exist; all of them follow a logic similar to the parliamentary system, where shareholders elect a board of directors (the parliament) who hires and fires the CEO (the prime minister).[23] When we talk of separation of powers in corporate governance, we mean a different thing: that the people who sit in the board are not supposed to be directly involved in management.[24]

The lack of variation, however, should not be a concern. Unlike national governments, companies were able to experiment with a much wider range of constitutional arrangements, and experiment they did. In FPT's database of companies before 1850, unincorporated companies had extreme freedom to select a variety of governance arrangements. Most elected their board of directors through shareholders elections, but some did not. Some had scores of directors, some had very few, and at least one had just a single director. Some directors served for life, and some had periodic elections. Some directors were elected by the shareholders and some by other members of the board. FPT show

---

[23] To be sure, a "monarchical" model for businesses, whereby a family is the ultimate authority for all decisions, is ubiquitous all over the world. The absence of a presidential model, however, is still telling.

[24] Lurie and Frenkel (2003), for example, write that "the new Israeli company law has adopted, in general terms, the democratic model and the principle of separation of powers for the governance of corporations, based on the view that a corporation is like a quasi-state, and thus should have a policy of checks and balances." But the authors stress that "corporate governance, as formulated within the context of the Israeli corporate law, is more like a parliamentary system."

that after much experimentation, companies tended to converge in their governance practices.

What did exist was a role for shareholders to appoint and dismiss salaried officers, including managers. FPT estimate that between 1720 and 1789, 70% of British companies allowed shareholder rights over appointment of managers. By 1844, that percentage had declined to around 50%. According to FPT, "the decline of shareholder rights over company employees was a significant element in the reconfiguration of the power relations within the companies that took place in these years. The G[eneral] M[eeting] shifted from being the source of all power in the company to performing a more closely specified and restricted role within a broader system of checks and balances, characterized by directorial oversight of management and GM oversight of the board." In other words, to the extent that there ever were similarities between corporate organizations and presidential systems, the companies that adopted those organizations went extinct or reformed, failing the market test.

As said above, there is scant evidence that widely held companies ever chose to have a full presidential system where shareholders would pick a CEO independently of the board of directors and one could not fire the other. And just like the dog that did not bark in Sherlock Holmes's story, this absence speaks volumes. You do not have to be the most radical proponent of the efficient market hypothesis to see that the business world would be in the best position to adopt any arrangement of better governance because it is more flexible and has more competitive pressure.

1.2.3 Local government

As is clear by now, the presidential and parliamentary governance structures may be applied to any effort to organize collective interests. Local government is an area where there is much variation. The most studied are cities in the US. Since the beginning of the 20th century, cities can—and increasingly have—adopted the "council–manager" model of government, whereby citizens elect a council, which in turn is responsible for choosing a city manager in charge of administration. This model stands in contrast with cities that adopt the "strong mayor" model, where citizens elect the mayor and council separately and the mayor is largely responsible for administration. The relationship between council–manager forms and parliamentary systems and strong mayor forms and presidential systems is widely recognized (Buisseret, 2016; Frederickson, Johnson, and Wood, 2004; Saha, 2008; Coate and Knight, 2011; Blume, Döring, and Voigt, 2011).

A review of the literature by Carr (2015) on the different outcomes of strong mayors versus city managers reveals a clear advantage for managers, which may not be immediately obvious from the academic style of writing:

> *The proposition that the council manager form of government produces better operational performance than mayor–council government has not received serious attention in the vast empirical literature on municipal government in the United States. [...] The empirical literature shows that council manager governments seek to distribute the benefits of public policies more broadly and experience lower voter turnout, and their senior executive officials direct more of their time to their roles as managers than is the case in mayor–council governments. [...] The evidence also suggests that council manager governments favor more comprehensive policy solutions, experience less conflict among senior officials, and are more willing to adopt innovative policies and practices than mayor–council governments. [...] Currently, the empirical literature does not support contentions that there are systematic differences between the two forms of government in their responsiveness to powerful local constituencies, in the levels and form of civic and political participation by residents (other than voting), in the quality of public services delivered, or in the general operational effectiveness of the organizations.*

What can be stressed from this excerpt is that for every objective measure that could be investigated, the results were either in favor of the council–manager model or a difference could not be found. Considering this, there are three possible positions we can take. First, we can conclude that there is probably no advantage for the council–manager system and this is merely the result of randomness. This conclusion seems far-fetched, as there are a number of studies significant enough to suggest that there really is some effect. Given all of the theory and evidence from other areas that we have seen, which points to the same direction, the probability of a fluke decreases.

Second, we can also take these results at face value and conclude that the manager system is associated with various good outcomes but not with "the quality of public services delivered, or in the general operational effectiveness of the organizations" as the passage above by Carr (2015) implies. However, taking this position would be odd. Having a different form of government would lead to a number of different outcomes, but regarding the quality of the services and operational effectiveness, for unexplained reasons, the outcomes would be comparable. Last, we can conclude that the quality and operational effectiveness are also related to the form of government just as much as the other, more objective measures, but studies have not been able to capture this yet.

The latter position should be preferred. If we look into how the studies that investigated how quality and general effectiveness were designed, we see that they were subject to several limitations. With respect to quality, there are three studies examined, and they all rely on surveys. The first study (Eskridge, 2012) asks mayors and managers from random cities in all 50 US states for their views on the quality of city services; mayors report better quality than managers. The second study (Ihrke, 2002) asks council members in New York and Wisconsin similar questions; in New York, council members indeed prefer the manager system, and in Wisconsin there is no statistically significant difference. The last study by Wood and Fan (2008) does not really address the differences between mayor–council and council–manager cities, so it actually does not contribute to the issue at hand.

With respect to effectiveness, the review by Carr (2015) examines four studies. The first study (Svara, 2002) asks council members how they evaluate their own effectiveness, and the officials rate it higher in council–manager cities than in mayor–council cities. The second study (Kreft, 2003) finds that house prices are higher in Ohio council–manager cities than in mayor–council cities, after several controls. The third study (MacDonald, 2006) does the same for Florida but does not find significant differences. The last study (Ha and Feiock, 2012) finds that "as predicted, mayor–council governments apply fiscal analyses less often, and local governments with an appointed administrators position apply fiscal analyses more often." We see, then, that even in the "inconclusive" areas, there is evidence in favor of council–managers. The only people who seem to evaluate mayors better than managers are mayors themselves, which is perhaps not surprising.

Other studies, not in the review, further provide evidence in favor of indirect appointment by the council. For example, Vlaicu and Whalley (2016) find that managers reduce spending in police forces without losing quality. Jensen, Malesky, and Walsh (2015) find there is less wasteful tax exemptions in manager cities, and Whalley (2013) finds that treasurers appointed by the council, as opposed to elected, borrow at lower rates. Jimenez (2019) finds that "council–manager cities have stronger budgetary solvency compared with mayor–council cities," and Nelson and Afonso (2019) find that council–manager cities have less corruption.

2

Can All of This Be True?

As mentioned in the introduction, the case for parliamentarism is made more difficult because of the almost consensual view that any generalizations are bound to fail. This consensus involves four closely related arguments: development is hard, we have tried all of the "quick fixes" already, development must come from within, and solutions are not interchangeable.

2.1   Development is not as hard as implied

Further development cannot be that hard to obtain after the Industrial Revolution. For all the talk about how rare and exceptional each development episode is, it is in fact a surprisingly common feature of modernity. Many readers will be familiar with the "hockey stick" of economic growth, which we reproduce below in Figure 2.1 for the UK. The figure shows that for centuries, the rate of per capita growth was very slow, and then it started to increase very fast in the 19th century.

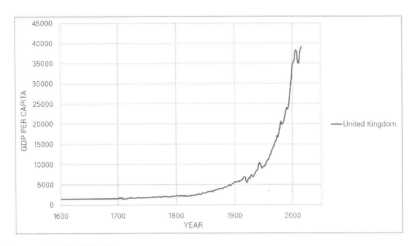

Source: Our World in Data

Figure 2.1 History's hockey stick – United Kingdom

The UK is not so exceptional. Many countries have embarked on a trajectory of sustained GDP per capita growth—not necessarily parliamentary—with an even more accelerated path. The figure below plots data relative to Japan, Italy, China, and India (compared to the UK).

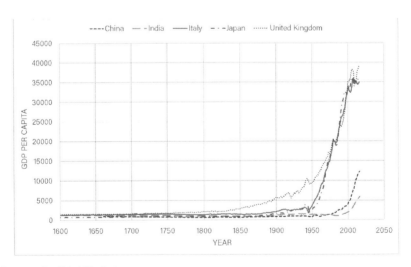

Source: Our World in Data

Figure 2.2 History's hockey stick - China, India, Italy, Japan, and United Kingdom

We see that sustained growth only happened in the last 200 years. This period might seem like a long time for any given person, but in terms of institutional changes—which is what I am proposing here—it is a very short period. We talk about the "Cambrian Explosion." This event lasted for 20 million years. Considering, however, that nothing like it happened for the billions of years before, "explosion" is an appropriate word. If development was as difficult as often argued, how could anyone explain the numerous success stories given how infrequent constitutional changes are? Perhaps the shortest list of developed countries are members of the Organisation for Economic Cooperation and Development's (OECD) Development Assistance Committee, with 29 members. That number represents almost 15% of the total number of countries. If 15% of the members of any given group have achieved an objective in a fraction of the time these group members have existed[25], one could hardly say the objective is elusive.

The word "hard" may sound objective but is in fact a value-ridden concept. I find solving the Rubik's Cube hard, but I know my brother can do it quite easily, and I have seen competitions where they solve it in seconds. If, on the other hand, someone tells me their dream is to pursue a career in engineering but is afraid that linear algebra, specifically, is too hard, I will tell them it is easy. These examples intuitively show that what is hard or not depends on the expected payoff. I do not give that much importance to learning how to solve the Rubik's Cube, so I say it is hard in the sense that it is not worth the effort. Conversely, linear algebra, something one must put a lot of effort into learning, is indeed easy if that is what is standing between you and an engineering degree. Given that economic development is the very best thing that can happen to a country, the amount of effort needed for it not to be worth pursuing would have to be astronomical. Humankind has not come close to putting enough effort into development.

---

[25] Most of the countries in the world have not existed for centuries. However, people have inhabited all corners of the globe for millennia, and they have always strived for nutrition, comfort, security, and health, which modern societies provide with much greater abundance.

2.2 We have not tried everything

If a child is stuck on a video game level that they find particularly hard, she will always say, "but I've tried everything." This makes sense, as we can only assess if we are spending more effort on something than it is worth after we have tried several different approaches that might solve the problem at hand. But when it comes to development, we have not tried almost anything. Currently, foreign aid amounts to around 0.2% (Page and Pande, 2018) of the world's GDP, which, given the stakes, does not really count as trying, even if all foreign aid spending was considered as properly trying to achieve development in recipient countries. But as has been demonstrated by development critics, a large part of this issue is not really development aid at all but rather the financing of military allies. A big percentage of what is actual development aid goes to programs that have been examined and failed to show they work, and a large amount of the programs that have been shown to work are only marginally important (Pritchett, 2018).

I must clarify what I mean by "failed to show they work." In development lingo, projects have expected "outputs" and expected "outcomes." The output is what the project is directly designed to do: build a hospital or a bridge, enroll X number of students in schools, vaccinate X many children, etc. The outcome, or impact, is the final objective—to increase economic activity, the literacy rate, life expectancy, or development in general. In the sense of achieving outputs, foreign aid mostly works. Maybe it is less efficient than it could be, but bridges get built, students get enrolled, and children get vaccinated. What critics mean when they claim that aid "does not work" is that the desired outcomes do not materialize, which implies the "theory of change" is wrong, and thus we need better theories of change.

However, the resources devoted to finding out "what works in development" are really small. The UK has spent only 0.9% of its foreign aid budget on research and development (R&D) (Lomborg, 2017). If we apply this to the world level—an optimistic assumption—it would correspond to 0.0018% of the world's GDP—or US$1.5 billion—which are explicitly dedicated to knowing what works or not. Lomborg estimates, however, that research for development could be one of the most effective ways to spend money. For comparison, leading countries in R&D spending like Germany and the US devote around 3% of their GDP to R&D. Journalist Rani Molla reports that Amazon alone spent US$23 billion in 2017,[26] which amounts to around 13% of their revenues.[27] Given that companies, which are behind most of this spending, know how to generate economic value in many ways while there exists an admitted lack of knowledge on how to promote development, we would expect the share of expenses devoted to R&D in development to be much greater than 0.9%.

Has parliamentarism been tried extensively? In statistics, it is common practice to distinguish between the "treatment" effect and the "intent to treat" effect. Using this distinction, we can talk of two forms of "trying" parliamentarism. In the first sense, we mean the actual adoption of parliamentary constitutions or de facto parliamentary governments. In the second sense, we mean the active promotion of parliamentary systems around the world. To both questions, the answer would be no; parliamentarism has not been thoroughly tried. First, most countries that adopt presidentialism never switch to parliamentarism. This is the case in the majority of countries in Latin America, which were never parliamentary. In the case of Africa, several countries, influenced by their former colonizers, adopted a parliamentary system for too few years before turning to presidentialism in what Robinson and Torvik (2016) call "endogenous presidentialism," mentioned above. Robinson and Torvik argue that the possibility of having greater personal control over society, offered by presidentialism, made leaders move away from parliamentary systems soon after they negotiated the departure of their European colonizers.

Second, there has never been a worldwide effort to promote parliamentary systems. The World Bank, the International Monetary Fund (IMF), and other international financial institutions do not promote

---

[26] https://www.vox.com/2018/4/9/17204004/amazon-research-development-rd
[27] The more proper comparison to GDP would not be revenues but value added by Amazon, which would be lower than their US$177 billion revenues in 2017, making R&D investment even larger in comparison.

parliamentary systems.[28] There is an Inter-parliamentary Union (IPU), but the richest country in the world, the US, is not even a member. The approved budget of the IPU for 2020 is around US$18 million. A sign of hope is that the UN adopted a resolution in 2018, establishing a partnership with the IPU and creating the International Day of Parliamentarism, celebrated for the first time on June 30, 2018.

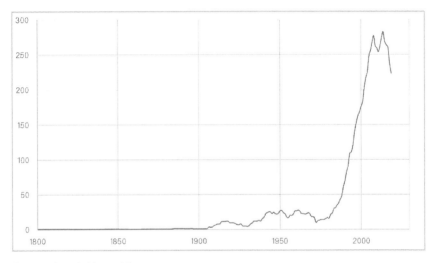

Source: Google Ngram Viewer

Figure 2.3 Ratio of "promotion of democracy" to "promotion of parliamentary" in English language books

If we look at references to the promotion of democracy and parliamentary systems, we find that the promotion of democracy started to have great advantage over parliamentary systems in the beginning of the 20th century.[29] A search of the Google Ngram Viewer, a tool which documents the relative occurrence of words in millions of English language books over time, for the expressions "promotion of democracy" and "promotion of parliamentary" (which includes expressions such as

---

[28] One could argue they are barred from doing it because of provisions in their articles of agreement; it is still true that they do not promote it, which is the point here.

[29] Earlier versions of this text mentioned different data. This is due to the Ngram Viewer tool updating their numbers.

"promotion of parliamentary democracy," "parliamentary monarchy," or "parliamentary systems") reveals how much more we promote democracy as compared to parliamentary systems.[30] The gap significantly grew, and in 2019, there were 223 as many references to "promotion of democracy" as to "promotion of parliamentary" in English language books, with a record of 282 in 2014.

2.3 Development does not have to come "from within"

I now turn to the claim that development must come from within, as argued, for example, by Andrews, Pritchett, and Woolcock (2017). According to this idea, only the internal forces of a society can determine if it will be developed or not. Outside activities are futile at best or are harmful at worst. This is an appealing idea. At first, it seems more flattering to the populations of developing countries. According to this narrative, these populations would take control of their own development instead of relying on others. Also, it is very easy to observe the many instances of disastrous foreign interference, supposedly well intentioned, in a variety of countries. Colonization and foreign invasion immediately come to mind, but negative foreign interference goes beyond full invasion or colonization. For example, the Cold War divided countries into US and Soviet spheres of influence; neither of the two powers seemed particularly keen in promoting democratic institutions in that period, and their development record is disappointing.

But the argument above only proves that foreign participation is not a sufficient condition for development. It does not prove it is not a necessary, or an enabling, condition and certainly does not prove that all foreign influence is harmful for development. Even a quick look at development episodes would show their dependence on foreign contacts. If we accept that institutions—broadly defined—are the main source

---

[30] The expression "promotion of parliamentarism" is not as widely used and simply does not appear in search results. The expression "promotion of parliamentary" will actually overestimate references to the promotion of parliamentary systems, because it will include indirectly related phrases such as "promotion of parliamentary diplomacy."

of development, then it is easy to observe the dependence they have on foreign contact. The most developed countries are concentrated in Europe, were settled by Europeans, or emulated European institutions. I can imagine you arguing "but all countries in the world fit this description." This is true, but the greater the interaction a country had with other developed countries, whether by trade, migration, investment, or culture, the greater the chance it would also become developed. Currently, at the OECD, the richest countries in the world have their own forum meant to harmonize their institutions according to what they see as the best practices. Symptomatically, the OECD is often called "the rich countries' club."

We have evidence that the output of democracy promotion is being achieved through international organizations' programs. As Finkel, Pérez-Liñán, and Seligson (2007) say, "contrary to the generally negative conclusions from previous research, there are clear and consistent impacts of USAID democracy assistance on democratization in recipient countries. An investment of one million dollars (measured in constant 2000 dollars) would foster an increase in democracy 65% greater than the change expected for the average country in the sample." Of course, that is an average and countries differ in many ways, but the size of the effect is still striking (so much so that some find it implausible, even if the direction of the effect might be correct). There is no reason to believe that promoting democracy must be so much more effective than promoting parliamentary systems. If anything, it is probably less traumatic for a leader of a strong presidential regime to cede power to the parliament then to a president of the opposition.

The point is not to argue for a development process that does not involve the local population; that would be completely silly. The point is to recognize that nobody should have to reinvent the wheel all of the time; there is a lot to be learned from other countries. If you think this is an exaggeration, I have an illustrative anecdote. When I was a graduate student, I attended a presentation by Bill Easterly, a former World Bank economist and current New York University professor who rose to prominence with the symptomatically named book *The Elusive Quest for Growth*. Given my interest in the subject, I was excited about his proposals. However, when the presentation turned to the suggestions segment, all we saw was a blank slide. Easterly's point was that there was nothing that the public in that room (some of them students from developed countries but many of them students from developing countries like myself) could learn from the world's top economists and apply in their attempts at helping to develop their home countries. To Easterly's credit, he has been publishing new findings (Easterly, 2019) showing that "Washington Consensus" policies, forever criticized as the quintessential package of ineffective, top-down, harmful measures, actually promoted a lot of good.

A closer examination reveals that the "development is extremely hard" and the "it must come from within" beliefs are actually contradictory. Even if development is not so hard that we cannot find what mechanisms explain it, it is not so easy that societies discover and rediscover this process repeatedly.[31] A look at the history of how major innovations spread shows it almost never happens through independent invention. Double-entry bookkeeping, for example, is considered instrumental for the spread of capitalism. Its popularization did not happen after several businessmen independently discovered it; it spread across Europe first, and later the world, through Italian merchants.[32] Likewise, companies' boards of directors were not rediscovered several times; they were copied across the globe. Copying is the rule. A look at multilateral development banks' articles of agreements—the conventions that create these banks—reveals that these texts are all basically the same. Empirical research confirms the same is true for trade agreements (Allee and Elsig, 2019). If internal processes were in fact the most important factor for the development of good institutions, then we would expect to see countries with good institutions appear independent of one another. The extreme concentration of the most successful countries in Europe, which all seemed to have their "critical junctures" almost simultaneously in historical terms, presents an insurmountable challenge to this view.

---

[31] There is a parallel to the controversy regarding direct instruction. See Stockard, Wood, and Khoury (2018).
[32] Interestingly, it was developed independently in Korea during the Goryeo dynasty.

In regard to which approach is more respectful to developing countries' populations, I believe this should not be part of the argument; however, given that it is, the more respectful view is whatever the true one is. Suppose you approach a friend of yours who is doing very well for himself, and when you ask what is it that he did, he answers that it is a "process of self-discovery that I cannot convey in words and that each person must find for oneself." If that is indeed the case, he was being respectful to you. But if the secret to his professional success is that his parents taught some valued skill from an early age, like coding in Python, and he does not mention that, then his "process of self-discovery" would seem like an affectation once you discovered the truth.

2.4 Development solutions are very similar around the globe

What about the assertion that there is no single solution and solutions are context dependent? To say that what works in one country does not what work in another is not the same as saying that a country might be doing well with one arrangement and another country doing well with another arrangement. The latter phenomenon is very common and usually means the arrangement is not decisive for successful outcomes. For example, people drive on the left side of the road in the UK, and the country does very well by international standards. They drive on the right side of the road in France, also very successful. What the "no single solution" assertion implies is that if we were to implement an arrangement in two different societies, in the society that came up with it and in a second society, the first society would be better off and the second would be worse off. That is sometimes true, but an examination of the world's most successful countries shows a large degree of convergence in their arrangements—not only on parliamentary democracy, as is our focus, but also in an array of other issues. This convergence is actively pursued by organizations such as the European Union (EU) and the OECD. Good arrangements are hard to come up with intellectually and are hard to implement politically. One you found one, you might as well spread it.

Berkowitz, Pistor, and Richard (2003) do find a "transplant effect," a tendency for a lower application of legal rules adopted from very different legislations, as compared to more similar legislations. But that effect only demonstrates that solutions are sometimes context dependent, not that they are always context dependent. The reader probably would not dispute that general vaccinations or the protection of property rights are universally applicable policies.[33] In fact, few people are consistent in applying this objection. An array of rules are expected to be universally applicable, most notably the UN Declaration on Human Rights. Closer to our issue, the promotion of democracy, in various forms, is usually seen as a valid endeavor. Why does the "no single solution" argument then not apply to these universally cherished solutions? Surely, it should.

Notably, Berkowitz Pistor, and Richard's (2003) own study on transplant effects find that the losses derived from adopting "foreign" legislation are dominated by the benefits of joining the OECD, a forum specifically created to "seek solutions to common problems." Whatever the losses involved in adopting foreign institutions are more than compensated by adopting the very best foreign institutions.

---

[33] If, on the other hand, the reader is a socialist who does not think that property rights are universally applicable, then it is probably the case that they believe a ban on property rights is universally applicable. Thus the thesis still holds.

3

What Do You Even Mean by "Parliamentary" or "Presidential"?

Does it make sense to call France parliamentary when they obviously have a president? Is it not the case that what countries practice is very different from their constitutions? Constitutions can vary significantly, and some countries do not even have a written constitution, like the UK. When I had to classify countries for the tables above (see footnote 6), I used the executive selection method with minimal levels of electoral participation, but I do not argue that this is the essential characteristic of parliamentarism; it is merely a proxy I used.

While there is indeed a lot of variation and different definitions, there is broad agreement about which countries are parliamentary and which countries are presidential. Lijphart (1994) identifies three main elements that countries must have to be considered pure parliamentary (versus pure presidential): an executive selected by the legislature (by the voters in the presidential case), an executive dependent on legislative confidence, and a collegial executive. This classification already admits eight different arrangements, but in practice these different arrangements do not significantly change most countries' classification.

The studies discussed above do not all use the same classification. McManus and Ozkan (2018), for example, use definitions based on the existence of the confidence vote. Roberts (2015) in turn uses the executive selection method to define a country as presidential or parliament based as long as there are contested elections. He avoids the term "parliamentary" to avoid confusion with the definition based on confidence. So, for example, Switzerland has a presidential system in Persson and Tabellini (2005) but a parliament-based one in Roberts. Poguntke and Webb (2005), in turn, convincingly show that even countries that can definitely be classified as presidential or parliamentary can have characteristics that conform to either of the models (such as personalization level, plebiscitary nature, etc.).

I instead treat all of these approaches as studying the same phenomenon, the differences between parliamentary and presidential systems, but through different lenses—by how much each country conforms to the "pure presidential" or the "pure parliamentary" model. *The main theme is executive subordination to parliament.* However, there is no "cutoff" point (or the literature is not unequivocal about it) that makes a country definitely presidential or definitely parliamentary, in the same way that there is no cutoff point that divides countries into democracies or autocracies. This does not—neither it should—stop academics from studying the phenomenon of democracy by relying on different forms of dichotomous classifications. Likewise, parliamentary and presidential categories are very useful.

I am taking a normative view here, which is clear from the title of the book. For our purposes, it does not really matter what the single most important aspect of parliamentary systems is that make them better; given how high the stakes are, countries would do well in adopting all of them. At the very least, there is no reason not to have parliaments both appoint and dismiss the government. The quirky solution is separating those functions; the burden of proof lies squarely with the proponents of that idea[34]. As Lijphart (1994) stresses, most countries do adopt one of the "pure" forms already, and there is no convincing evidence that a mixed regime is better than a pure parliamentary form. Failing to make a recommendation because we are not certain about which of Lijphart's element is the most important would be an instance of the "inflation of conflict" fallacy, a type of continuum fallacy:

> [A] form of [inflation of conflict] correctly points to disagreement in a field but incorrectly implies that, as a result, little can be known. One scientist might claim that the Earth is 4.5 billion years old and another that its age is 4.6 billion years. The arguer then concludes that therefore we really have no idea of the age of the Earth. These scientists, though, are in fundamental agreement on the age of the Earth. More work may reveal whose estimate is more accurate, but the disagreement is minor. (Wible, 2018)

3.1 Attenuation bias

The uncertainty on how to classify countries as parliamentary or presidential in effect points to an even larger effect of parliamentary systems because of attenuation bias. When the data are noisy, there is a larger risk of spurious relationships. This means that there would seem to exist a relationship between two variables (in this case, government form and development outcomes), but in fact the relationship would be elusive and only due to random variation. But if you can discard the hypothesis of a spurious correlation (and I argue that indeed this can be discarded), then whatever uncertainty that is in your independent or explanatory variable measurement biases the estimate of the impact on the dependent or response variable, making it seem smaller than it really is.

---

[34] Also, there is no reason to believe there is a particular order for adoption of elements of parliamentary systems. As far as we understand, the relationship is monotonic – the more parliamentary elements we have, the better. If it is more realistic to pursue one element before the other, that is fine; there does not seem to be reasons to fear a worsening of the situation. Parliamentary systems can be built like a beaver's dam, one log at a time.

To see the point, it is better to use an example. Suppose that two variables are perfectly related. My example will be time studying and test scores, even though, of course, the relationship is not perfect. Let us take four students from a class and take note of their correct scores and the correct amount of time studying.

Table 3.1 Accurate study time, accurate test scores

Student	Time studying	Score
A	1	1
B	1	1
C	3	3
D	3	3

This table can be plotted in the graph below:

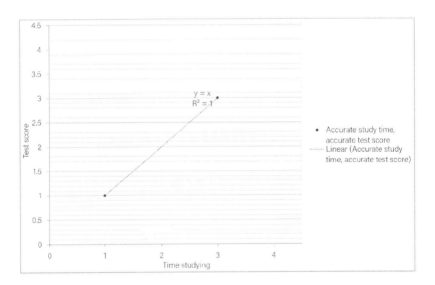

Figure 3.1 Accurate plot

Now suppose that the person copying the test scores to the table was particularly sloppy and got the scores wrong but with an equal chance of overestimating the scores and underestimating them. This is what the table could like if that were the case:

Table 3.2 Accurate study time, noisy test scores

Student	Time studying	Score
A	1	0
B	1	2
C	3	2
D	3	4

While it would seem that time studying explains less about test scores than is really the case (by construction, time studying explains 100% of test scores), the estimate of the slope would be unbiased, with the same value of 1:

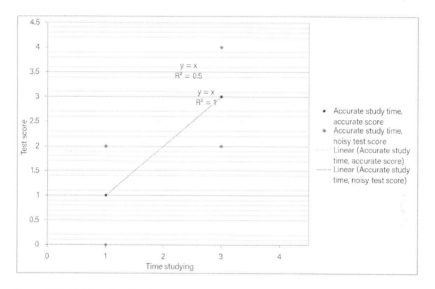

Figure 3.2 Unbiased estimate

We can see that the lines in the graph above—the accurate blue line and the noisy but unbiased orange line—perfectly overlap each other. Suppose, however, that the person creating the table was sloppy not when they wrote down the test scores but when they wrote down the study time. The logic, however, is the same: they get things wrong evenly. Here is the table:

Table 3.3 Noisy study time, accurate test score

Student	Time studying	Score
A	0	1
B	2	1
C	2	3
D	4	3

When we plot this, we get a different graph:

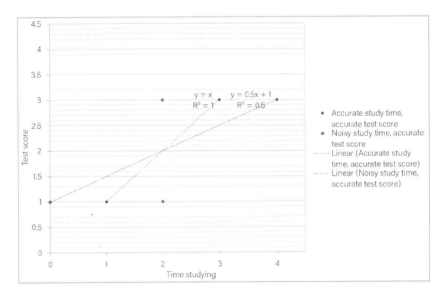

Figure 3.3 Attenuation bias

We see that when we get uncertain measures of the explanatory variable, the effect on the response variable seems smaller than it actually is. Applying this logic to the difficulty of determining a precise measure of parliamentarism versus presidentialism in different societies at different times, we would expect that the effect of parliamentarism on the positive outcomes is even greater than has been usually estimated.

You may still argue: what if we are being systematically biased against presidential systems? Suppose we instinctively associate presidential systems with bad outcomes and parliamentary systems with good outcomes, so we are more likely to classify a country as one or the other depending on the outcomes they already have. First, there is scant evidence this could be happening. Most studies cited above use objective classification of constitutional texts. Second, even if this was happening, the attenuation bias could be greater, not smaller.

To see why, suppose our biased person responsible to fill the table never took note of the time students studied in the first place. Instead, it is inferred from the grades. For those who had a grade of 1, they infer an amount of time studying of 0. For those who had a grade of 3, they assign a whopping amount of 6 to time studied.

Table 3.4 biased study time, accurate test score

Student	Time studying	Score
A	0	1
B	0	1
C	6	3
D	6	3

Below is the graphic representation of the table above:

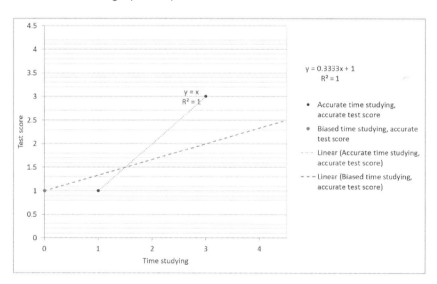

Figure 3.4 Attenuation bias for a biased data collection process

The attenuation bias now makes the relationship look much smaller than the true relationship. However we look at it, it seems clear that, to the extent there is uncertainty in the degree of parliamentarization of a country, it only makes us believe the effects should be even larger.

3.2 Beyond presidentialism and parliamentarism?

There are authors who believe the presidential-parliamentary classification is not as defining a feature for the workings of government as usually thought and that we should strive to go "beyond presidentialism and parliamentarism" (Cheibub, Elkins, and Ginsburg, 2014). This is a mistaken approach.

How do the authors conclude for "skepticism regarding the classical typology of presidentialism, parliamentarism and semi-presidentialism"? They examine the literature and find what constitutional characteristics some authors believe should be associated with each system of government (such as executive decree, veto power, etc.). Then they find that these characteristics are not as associated with their preferred classification of system of government as they deemed should be the case. In their words, "within-type cohesion is low (at least by our expectations)" (Cheibub, Elkins, and Ginsburg, 2014). Below, we see the table with the list of attributes that they will check for a correlation with system of government.

Table 3.5 Cheibub, Elkins and Ginsburg presumed attributes of executive-legislative Systems

Presumed Attributes of Executive-Legislative Systems			
	System		
Attribute	Presidential	Parliamentary	Semi-presidential
Defining attribute			
Assembly confidence	No	Yes	For head of govt
Popularly elected head of state	Yes	No	Yes
Elective attributes			
Executive decree	No	Yes	Depends

Presumed Attributes of Executive-Legislative Systems			
	System		
Attribute	**Presidential**	**Parliamentary**	**Semi-presidential**
Emergency powers	Strong	Weak	Strong
Initiation of legislation	Legislature	Executive	Depends
Legislation oversight	Yes	No	Depends
Executive veto	Yes	No	Depends
Cabinet appointment	Executive	Legislature	Depends
Other attributes			
Assembly dissolution*	No	Yes	Depends

The first problem with this approach is that it is not clear the authors are accurately interpreting the literature they cite. For example, they misinterpret Poguntke and Webb's (2005) introduction of a dimension of "presidentialization" and of "partification" *within* parliamentary, semi-presidential, and presidential forms of government. What Poguntke and Webb propose is that even when countries can be clearly classified as parliamentary, semi-presidential, or presidential from a constitutional point of view, they may still have extra-constitutional presidential or parliamentary elements. By this newly proposed dimension, a country may become more or less presidentialized even though their constitutional form of government did not change. Poguntke and Webb describe how the elements of this dimension are very related to form of government while still observing much variation within the systems.

Cheibub, Elkins, and Ginsburg (2014), however, write that "importantly, Poguntke and Webb's dimension of partified versus presidentialized government is *orthogonal*—theoretically and empirically—to the classic typology: all three types exhibit significant variation along this dimension" [emphasis added]. They include, in a footnote, the reference "Poguntke and Webb 2005, 6, *notably Figure 1.1*" (emphasis added). Recall that "orthogonal" in this context means "statistically independent." If that were the case, this is what Poguntke and Webb's figure should look like:

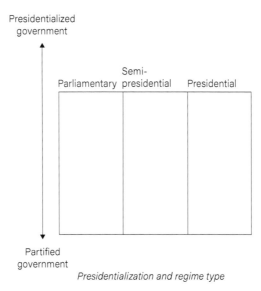

Presidentialization and regime type

Figure 3.5 What Poguntke and Webb's graph should look like if forms of government were orthogonal to the partified versus presidentialized dimension

Instead, this is what their Figure 1.1 looks like:

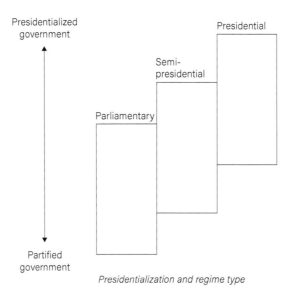

Presidentialization and regime type

Figure 3.6 Poguntke and Webb's graph as displayed in their book

We see that the form of government dimension is directly related to the "presidentialized" and "partified" dimensions that Poguntke and Webb (2005) describe. I went through the trouble of estimating the slope, and it is a little above 0.5. However, the graph is clearly made for illustrative purposes and is not meant to be taken literally. Despite the claim by Cheibub, Elkins, and Ginsburg (2014) that the dimensions are empirically unrelated, there is no direct empirical test of the thesis—for no less a reason than the fact that the only presidential country they study is the US.

When one looks at the indicators that Poguntke and Webb consider more important for the "presidentialized-partified" axis, the specific constitutional rules that are the object of Cheibub, Elkins, and Ginsburg (2014), such as initiation of legislation, executive decree, etc., are simply not there. Poguntke and Webb (2005) list as particularly relevant indicators characteristics that are much more abstract. Among others:

LEADERSHIP POWER WITHIN THE EXECUTIVE

- The growth of resources at the disposal of the chief executive

- Trends towards an integrated communication strategy controlled by the chief executive as a means of defining policy alternatives (which is a precondition for achieving desired decisions)

- Trends towards increasingly centralized control and coordination of policy-making by the chief executive: do we find evidence that the chief executive's office seeks greater coordinating control of the policy-making process?

- Trends towards more personal polling: do we find evidence that prime ministerial offices regularly monitor the personal popularity of leaders and voter policy preferences?

- A growing tendency of chief executives to appoint non-party technocrats or to promote rapidly politicians who lack a distinctive party power base

- A growing tendency to have more cabinet reshuffles while the prime ministers remains in office

- Prime ministers increasingly invoking a personalized mandate based on their electoral appeal, not least to control important decisions

  […]

LEADERSHIP POWER WITHIN THE PARTY

- Rule change which give party leaders more formal powers

- The growth of the leaders' offices in terms of funding and personnel

- The capacity of leaders to forge programmes autonomously of their parties

- The use of plebiscitary modes of political communication and mobilization. Do leader seek to bypass sub-leader or activist strata of the party by communicating directly with the grass roots in respect of programmatic or strategic questions?

- Evidence of personalized mandates in the sense of people becoming leading candidates despite not being the most senior party politicians (for instance, Blair rather than Brown, Schröder rather than Lafontaine, Rutelli rather than Amato, and so on)

The list by Poguntke and Webb is much more extensive and much more abstract than the very specific rules examined by Cheibub, Elkins, and Ginsburg (2014). More importantly, Poguntke and Webb's list seems much more consistently "presidential" than the other list. The first sees as evidence of presidentialization any trend toward greater power for presidents or individual leaders, which makes sense. The list by Cheibub, Elkins, and Ginsburg, on the other hand, is not as visibly linked to presidential systems or presidential powers. Why would a constitution that does *not* provide for executive decree be more presidential than one that does? Why is the initiation of legislation in the executive a mark of parliamentarization and not the opposite?

Reading Cheibub, Elkins, and Ginsburg (2014) increases the puzzle. The authors say that

While emergency powers are more typically associated with presidential constitutions, decree powers – in particular the scope of the permissible delegation of authority by parliament32 – has been more easily justified in the context of parliamentary regimes, even though it has been a concern in constitutions representing all regime types – parliamentary, presidential and semi-presidential. [...] Executive decree powers, [...] were justified in the European democracies of the interwar period by the argument that the transfer of legislative authority to the executive did not imply abdication, since parliament retained the power to withdraw confidence from the government and remove it from office. In this sense, decree power was seen as merely an issue of legal technique, changing parliamentary practice from ex ante to ex post approval of government act. [emphasis in the original]

We see, from the authors' own account, that executive decrees are not expected to be *empirically* more associated with parliamentary countries. The link is merely recommendatory. Given that in parliamentary countries the parliament has ultimate authority, executive decrees are not as dangerous as they are in a presidential country. The authors make a distinction between "emergency powers" and "decree powers". One is supposed to be exceptional and the other is a regular feature, but in practice they are the same thing. The fact that executive decrees are not rare in presidential countries is a reason for greater caution against presidentialism, not less. Perhaps the most notorious provision for emergency decrees is Article 48 of the Constitution of the German Weimar Republic, one of the destabilizing factors of 1930s Germany. As Evans (2005) puts it: "Article 48 of the Weimar constitution, in particular, which gave the President the power to rule by decree in time of emergency, had never been intended to be the basis for any more than purely interim measures; the Nazis made it into the basis for a permanent state of emergency that was more fictive than real and lasted in a technical sense all the way up to 1945."

Likewise, the authors write that "executives in presidential constitutions are far from being powerless when it comes to initiating legislation." I was not able to find in their text the source of the supposed conventional wisdom that executives in presidential constitutions are powerless to initiate legislation. The references they provide (Döring's 1996 Parliaments and Majority Rule in Western Europe, Huber's 1996 *Rationalizing Parliament*, and Lauvaux's 1988 *Parlementarism Rationalisé et Stabilité du Pouvoir Exécutif*) do not deal primarily with presidential systems. As in the case of executive decrees, why would giving the president the power to initiate legislation make a system *less* presidential?

The second problem is that the authors treat a failure to confirm a hypothesis as an indictment of the whole presidential-parliamentary classification, which is grounded on all of the theory, evidence, and lived experience that was discussed above. Is not the simpler explanation to suppose that those were not as important characteristics of systems of government as Cheibub, Elkins, and Ginsburg (2014) assumed?

Cheibub, Elkins, and Ginsburg (2014) use the example of animal taxonomy to talk about the complexities of classification. I will do the same. Suppose we elaborate a number of hypotheses about dinosaurs versus mammals—that dinosaurs are all extinct, are larger than mammals, and may be predators. Mammals, on the other hand, are not all extinct, are smaller than dinosaurs, and are scavengers. When I test my hypotheses, I find that none of them are confirmed. Not all dinosaurs are extinct; indeed, all birds are dinosaurs. Birds are, on average, smaller than mammals today. Many mammals are predators. Just like Cheibub, Elkins, and Ginsburg (2014), I may claim that the period of observation is a much more important determinant of the characteristics I am studying than the mammal-dinosaur divide. Should I abandon altogether my view that mammals and dinosaurs have meaningful differences, or should I perhaps use this evidence to refute my hypotheses? The latter should be preferred.

To be sure, Cheibub, Elkins, and Ginsburg (2014), despite their general skepticism of the typology, do not go as far as say that there are *no* meaningful differences. They write that "no one should doubt that the idea that the origin and survival of executives represents an important constitutional distinction. But it seems possible that this preoccupied scholars and constitution makers at the expense of dimensions of executive-legislative relations—dimensions that *may* be orthogonal to the classic distinction" (emphasis in the original, but I would have added them as well). Indeed, they may be orthogonal (and they may not). These dimensions may also be very important, they may not be, or they may rest in wrong assumptions, which is what I argue for above. But should this admitted possibility stop us from concluding anything about presidential versus parliamentary systems?[35] That would be a mistake.

---

[35]   I believe this may be perceived as a strawman: "no one said you cannot conclude *anything*." I would reply that I do not see any general conclusion about parliamentary versus presidential systems that Cheibub, Elkins and Ginsburg would subscribe to.

4

Why Not Parliamentarism?
Avoiding Fisher's Mistake

The curious associations with lung cancer found in relation to smoking habits do not, in the minds of some of us, lend themselves easily to the simple conclusion that the products of combustion reaching the surface of the bronchus induce, though after a long interval, the development of a cancer. If, for example, it were possible to infer that smoking cigarettes is a cause of this disease, it would equally be possible to infer on exactly similar grounds that inhaling cigarette smoke was a practice of considerable prophylactic value in preventing the disease, for the practice of inhaling is rarer among patients with cancer of the lung than with others. (Fisher, 1958)

I have spent quite a few pages making the case *for* parliamentarism. But you may still have doubts. One argument could be that the safest course of action would be no constitutional change until a "smoking gun" is provided. While it is usually a good principle not to promote changes until you have good reason, a lack of action in light of less than perfect information is a rarely followed rule, and when it is, the results can be disastrous.

Ronald Fisher is a towering figure in statistics and biological sciences, which is easily verified in his Wikipedia page. Richard Dawkins argues that Fisher was the greatest biologist since Darwin and explains that "not only was he the most original and constructive of the architects of the neo-Darwinian synthesis, Fisher also was the father of modern statistics and experimental design. He therefore could be said to have provided researchers in biology and medicine with their most important research tools, as well as with the modern version of biology's central theorem."[36] He also "was the founder of experimental agricultural research, saving millions from starvation through rational crop breeding programs" (Miller, 2000).

Fisher, however, was far from perfect.[37] One of his greatest mistakes was his stance on the smoking-cancer link. In Stolley's (1991) words,

Fisher developed four lines of argument in questioning the causal relation of lung cancer to smoking. I will first list these and then briefly describe the evidence he produced in support of these arguments.

1 *If A is associated with B, then not only is it possible that A causes B, but it is also possible that B is the cause of A. In other words, smoking may cause lung cancer, but it is a logical possibility that lung cancer causes smoking.*

2 *There may be a genetic predisposition to smoke (and that genetic predisposition is presumably also linked to lung cancer).*

3 *Smoking is unlikely to cause lung cancer because secular trend and other ecologic data do not support this relation.*

4 *Smoking does not cause lung cancer because inhalers are less likely to develop lung cancer than are noninhalers.*

---

[36] *https://www.edge.org/conversation/ armand_marie_leroi-who-is-the-greatest-biologist-of-all-time*

[37] His eugenics studies are the greatest stain on his record.

Stolley (1991), however, points out that

Fisher never produced any data or organized any study to follow up on this implausible hypothesis [i.e., a genetic predisposition to smoke]. It is also noteworthy that Fisher was a smoker himself. Part of his resistance to seeing the association may have been rooted in his own fondness for smoking and in his dislike of criticism of any part of his life. Fisher's data concerning the genetics of smoking are sparse indeed. In two letters to Nature, he presents some tables based on information he received from a Professor Verschuer of Germany and from Dr. Eliot Slater of London. There are no further details about these twin studies nor do we know how the smoking histories are obtained, categorized, or analyzed. He presents tables that the reader is expected to take at face value with almost no information about the study protocol or methods of investigation.

Fisher struggled to provide a better explanation for the link between smoking and cancer than the straightforward link: smoking causes cancer. His answer—a genetic predisposition—was far less satisfactory. Likewise, what is a more fitting explanation for why parliamentary countries fare so much better? We have seen that they do fare much better, and we have no reason to believe that development by itself, as measured by GDP growth, makes countries and other organizations parliamentary. So we are either explicit about what other factor is causing countries to become parliamentary and developed at the same time, or we assume the existence of some unknown factor that causes both. Either choice seems less warranted then the hypothesis that parliamentarism causes development.

Is it being European? It cannot be. First, Europe was not developed for millennia; second, parliamentarism is associated with good outcomes also outside of Europe. This means that being European cannot be a main driver for development and for parliamentarism (at least not without interaction with other aspects). Is it monarchies? Also not plausible. Monarchies have existed for a long time without producing anything close to good results (or giving rise to parliamentary government, for that matter), and parliamentary countries that are not monarchies fare very well. Common law? We are moving closer. The tradition of common law has characteristics of decentralization, and it is conceivable that it could give rise to the impersonalized form of government that is parliamentarism. But only a share of parliamentary countries adheres to common law—in Europe, land of parliaments, only the UK and Ireland do.

Urbanization is a better candidate. As economist Paul Romer puts it in a blog post[38], urbanization passes all four components of the "Pritchett Test" (as does parliamentarism, you will note):

Pritchett proposes a basic, four part test that economists could consider when someone claims that governments or donors should experiment with policies designed to promote variable X because more X is good for development:

In a cross-sectional comparison of levels, do countries that are more developed have more X?

In cross-sectional comparison of growth rates, do countries that have rapid growth in X also tend to experience a rapid increase in standards of living?

When we look at the few countries for which we have long historical records, do the ones that become much more developed also acquire much more X?

If we look for countries that switch from a regime of slow economic development to a regime of rapid development, do we see a parallel shift in the rate of growth of change in X?

The fact that urbanization passes the Pritchett Test means we have evidence that it is a major driver of development. We also have reasons

---

to believe that urbanization fosters parliamentarization. Abramson and Boix (2019) write that "those factors that started those processes of urbanization and proto-industrialization also generated social actors capable of forcing parliamentary checks (in the form of city councils or territorial assemblies with stronger urban representation) on would-be absolutists."

I do not dispute these statements. Urbanization may be an enabling or even a necessary condition for the strengthening of parliaments. But this does not mean that parliaments are merely a byproduct of urbanization that is largely inconsequential for development, nor do the authors argue that. In Abramson and Boix's (2019) own words,

Current institutional theories of growth grant institutions a primary causal role in economic development: a stable political order guaranteed by the state jointly with parliamentary institutions constraining the executive resulted in well-defined property rights and low transaction costs, fostering private investment, economic specialization, trade, and innovation. Here we do not deny that one or more of these institutions performed the functions attributed by the institutionalist literature. Our claim is, instead, that those political institutions were embedded in a broader process of economic and technological change.

This hypothesis can be visualized this way:

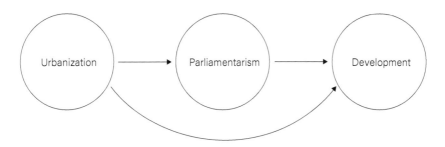

Figure 4.1   Abramson and Boix's thesis

The mere byproduct hypothesis, in turn, can be visualized like this:

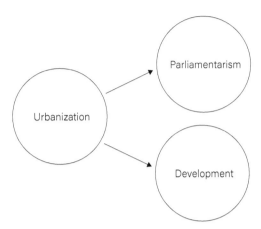

Figure 4.2 Parliamentarism as epiphenomenon

If this epiphenomenon hypothesis were true, we would not see the kinds of differences in all sorts of welfare indicators between countries with similar urbanization levels[39], and instead we would see much larger differences in welfare indicators between the rural and urban populations of a country[40]. What we do observe is that conditions from country to country vary dramatically, and sometimes the striking differences can be seen in neighboring cities at the border. Whatever inequality there exists inside of countries, it is much smaller than inequalities between countries[41]. As Acemoglu and Robinson (2012) make abundantly clear in *Why Nations Fail*, political conditions matter.

As a stretch, a critic could still argue that political institutions *are* one of the key drivers of development, along with urbanization. However, the key political institutions that are drivers of development are not related

---

[39] While countries with a very large rural to urban population fare worse, a large urban population without good institutions does not seem to bring about development. See Hommann and Lall (2019)

[40] In the United States, for example, median rural household income was 96% of median urban household income in 2015. *https://www.census.gov/newsroom/ blogs/random-samplings/2016/12/a_comparison_of_rura.html*

[41] *https://ourworldindata.org/global-economic-inequality*

to parliamentarism, which in turn *is* related to urbanization. The figure below may help us understand this last thesis.

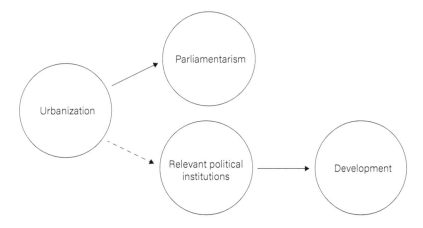

Figure 4.3   Political institutions matter, but not parliamentarism

The dashed arrow from "urbanization" to "relevant political institutions" tries to convey the idea that, according to this hypothesis, urbanization may or may not be related to the relevant political institutions in this framework, but parliamentarism is not a major force behind development. Is this possible? Certainly, just as it was perfectly possible that some genetic condition could cause a desire to smoke and, independently, lung cancer, as Fisher suggested, instead of the simple smoking causes cancer explanation. But at this stage of our knowledge, we do not have good reasons to believe that. We do, however, have many other independent reasons to believe parliamentary systems do better.

4.1   The risks of inaction

The comparison to Fisher's reluctance to accept the damaging effects of smoking is fit in more than one way. In that case, as in this one, excessive caution in implementing a change of course can mean tragic human costs. In the smoking case, the results are now known. Holford et al. (2014) give an estimate for the US, but we should expect similar results all over the world:

In 1964-2012, an estimated 17.7 million deaths were related to smoking, an estimated 8.0 million (credible range [CR], 7.4-8.3 million, for the lower and upper tobacco control counterfactuals, respectively) fewer premature smoking-related deaths than what would have occurred under the alternatives and thus associated with tobacco control (5.3 million [CR, 4.8-5.5 million] men and 2.7 million [CR, 2.5-2.7 million] women). This resulted in an estimated 157 million years (CR, 139-165 million) of life saved, a mean of 19.6 years for each beneficiary (111 million [CR, 97-117 million] for men, 46 million [CR, 42-48 million] for women). During this time, estimated life expectancy at age 40 years increased 7.8 years for men and 5.4 years for women, of which tobacco control is associated with 2.3 years (CR, 1.8-2.5) (30% [CR, 23%-32%]) of the increase for men and 1.6 years (CR, 1.4-1.7) (29% [CR, 25%-32%]) for women.

What would have happened if we had waited for the kind of evidence that Fisher demanded? A randomized controlled trial, even if it was considered ethical—a big if—even if it was logistically possible—also doubtful—would take decades to produce results. Most likely, we would still not have an answer.

Likewise, can we expect to have a definitive answer to the question on the superiority of forms of government anytime soon? I do not think so. For good or ill, randomized controlled trials are increasingly becoming the "gold standard" of research. Like in the smoking case, however, it is hard to imagine a convincing study in the next few years that would be both practical and considered ethical. In any case, the results would take many years to appear. How long will we have to wait? What would be the costs?

4.2 The risks of action

This analysis would be not be balanced if I talked about the risks of inaction but not of the risks of action. Many writers might avoid this part because it presents two very unattractive choices: 1) deny the existence of risks altogether or 2) admit that there are risks but that the expected benefits compensate them, and be prepared for that concession to be used as a reason to completely dismiss the whole argumentation. This is due to the effect that availability bias has on risk perception (Sunstein, 2011). I will take my chances with the second option.

One way to think more coherently about risks is to compare it with other things we are already doing and perceive it to be safe enough. I am proposing a change in legislations, constitutions, and practices. What would be the possible reaction to this? How would people react to the costs associated with the transition, even if the benefits probably outweigh the costs?

My first comparison will, once again, be with anti-smoking policies. In 2020, the amount of people smoking in the countries I have lived in—Brazil and the US—is relatively small, and anti-smoking rules seem to be effortlessly enforced. People have become used to not being able to smoke anywhere inside of office buildings, shopping malls, and restaurants. But this was not as easy a process as it may seem today. Deeply ingrained habits in a very large share of the population had to be changed. The reason why the anti-smoking campaign was so successful is that many people did give up smoking altogether, not that they stopped smoking around others. While secondhand smoking health effects are terrible, they respond to a little over 10% of smoking-related deaths.[42]

When I was a child in the 1980s (or even a teenager in the 1990s), the world looked very different. In those days, there was a smoking section inside of airplanes, without any real barrier to stop the smoke from flowing from one section to the other. Smoking was common in restaurants, hospitals, and high school classrooms. Many smokers deeply resented the anti-smoking campaigns and the increasing limitations of areas

---

[42] "Most of the 20 million smoking-related deaths since 1964 have been adults with a history of smoking; however, 2.5 million of those deaths have been among nonsmokers who died from diseases caused by exposure to secondhand smoke." See https://www.hhs.gov/surgeongeneral/reports-and-publications/tobacco/consequences-smoking-factsheet/index.html#:~:text=Most%20of%20the%2020%20million,by%20exposure%20to%20secondhand%20smoke.

where smoking was allowed. Many smokers attached their identity to cigarettes, and the association with sex appeal was frequently explored. Whole countries would be judged on how tolerant they were toward smokers. France and Argentina seemed to be beloved by the smoker lot.

Still, governments all over the world acted. They did not let a fear of a revolt of the smokers stop them from doing what made sense from a health point of view. They were not afraid that black markets could poison political institutions (perhaps a rational fear given the history of prohibition). Should they have? Recall that, as mentioned above, anti-smoking policies are responsible for saving around 157 million years of life in the US alone (Holford et al., 2014). Even if you are a Spock-like cost-benefit policy evaluator (or perhaps, particularly if so), the benefits of such measures are massive. I will use US$100,000 per quality-adjusted life year (QALY), which is close to usual estimates (Neumann and Cohen, 2018). A simple multiplication of the dollar value of a QALY with the number of years of lives saved gives us a total benefit of US$16 trillion.

My second example will be much more related to the current times. As of this writing, millions are working from home. Schools, restaurants, and theaters are closed or operating with very limited capacity. A few months ago, there were stay-at-home orders, which gave the police the power to prosecute those who left their houses without a valid reason[43]. These efforts were taken in order to save lives and to try to prevent a chaotic response to a deadly and contagious virus. The amount of intrusion in the world's populations livelihoods has no comparison since World War II. Governments all over the world still acted, not because they believed there were no risks in doing what they are doing—an untenable position—but because they believe the risks of not doing anything were greater.

What are the risks of adopting parliamentary systems all over the world? By themselves, parliamentary constitutions, even if one is still not convinced of their superiority, are most definitely not very dangerous.

---

[43] https://www.usatoday.com/story/news/politics/2020/04/16/
coronavirus-arrests-rise-police-enforce-stay-home-orders-states/5142415002/

The idea that a country would be at great risk of collapse *because* it has a parliamentary constitution instead of a presidential one would need an extraordinary amount of evidence to be credible. I could not find a well-known modern source that would make such a claim. As already mentioned, even for a sitting president, it is arguably safer to hand power over to parliament than to a president from an opposing group.

Perhaps the risks would derive not from the system itself but by how it would be received by a population that is too attached to the presidential system of government. While more credible than the first hypothesis, it is still doubtful that the mere proposal and eventual legitimate approval of parliamentary government in presidential countries would be met with more resistance than the measures discussed above. Although we consistently think otherwise, the vast majority of people do not know nor care about their system of government. Even if they did know the details and cared, would they care about it more than they care about smoking if they are smokers? Or about leaving their houses, celebrating weddings, or attending their families' funerals—all restricted during the COVID-19 pandemic? If your reflex is to respond by stressing the risks of *not* taking those risky measures with respect to smoking or COVID-19, remember that the risks of inaction with respect to systems of government have been discussed as well, and they are far from trivial.

4.3 Wrapping up Fisher's mistake

The comparison to Fisher's mistake in the case of smoking and cancer is not merely a cautionary tale. Anecdotes can be valuable, but it is often the case that for every anecdote that points to one direction, you will find another that points to the opposite direction. This particular mistake by Fisher is actually an instance of a general mistake Fisher consistently made, his denial of Bayesian statistics. "If Bayes story were a TV melodrama, it would need a clear-cut villain, and Fisher would probably be the audience's choice by acclamation" (McGrayne, 2011).

5

A Bayesian Estimate—
The Weight of Concurrent Evidence

In the beginning of this book, I said that no piece of evidence by itself is convincing but instead, all pieces of evidence make a very convincing case indeed. In this chapter, I make this assertion more concrete by means of a Bayesian estimate of the probability that the hypothesis that parliamentary systems matter for good outcomes is correct. The following is a brief explanation of Bayesian analysis by Aksoy and Guner (2015):

In Bayesian analysis the new information is combined with the previously available information. At this point the prior information (distribution) corresponds to the historical data or the subjective thought of the decision maker about the unknown parameter of the involved process. The consequential decision or inferential statement (posterior distribution) combined all available information about the uncertain parameter of the process. The performance of the succeeding updates depends on the prior information therefore the determination of prior information is significant. If there is not any basis of the prior information then the decision maker may consider the non-informative priors about the random variable which represents the unknown parameter may obtain any value in its domain evenly likely (Hill, 1997, 1999; Shih, 2001; Winkler, 2003). Bayesian update process can be described using three distinct probability distributions; prior, likelihood and posterior probabilities:

- *Prior probability represents our knowledge before we observe evidence. The prior probability of an event A is expressed as P (A).*

- *Likelihood represents a factor that is used to update our prior knowledge. The likelihood for an event A and an evidence B is expressed in terms of a conditional probability P(B|A).*

- *Posterior represents combined probability of initial probability and additional information from the process. The posterior probability of an event A given the evidence B is expressed in terms of a conditional probability P(A|B).*

In the Bayesian approach, forecasters update their knowledge in response to an observed event iteratively. This process is depicted in Figure[5.1] (note: Figure 1 in their text).

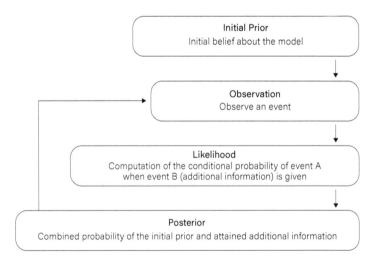

Figure 5.1 Bayesian update model

In summary, Bayes's theorem can be expressed as

$$P(A|B) = \frac{P(B|A)P(A)}{P(B)}$$

Bayes's theorem makes many people uncomfortable because priors need to be established, and these always come from best guesses. Guessing means that we lose the precision of a p-value derived from rigorous definitions. However, the estimates we arrive at are much more reliable than taking a p-value as a correct representation of reality. A strip from xkcd, a math-oriented webcomic, can illustrate this better[44]:

Source: xkcd.com/1132

Figure 5.2 Frequentists versus Bayesians (comic #1132)

The strip's "Bayesian statistician" does not know exactly the probability of the sun exploding at any moment. However, he knows that it is

---

[44] There is a long online discussion on whether the xkcd comic portrayal is fair. The comic author himself apologized to frequentist statisticians for a possible misrepresentation of how they think about statistics. For our purposes, however, if you are using the findings of the separate studies we have talked about and not adjusting priors for evaluating the relative probability that parliamentarism is superior, then the caricature of a frequentist does apply. Andrew Gelman suggests that it would have been better to call the "frequentist" statistician a "rote statistician" and the "Bayesian" a "sensible statistician," which I deem reasonable. See *https://web.archive.org/web/20130117080920/http://andrewgelman.com/2012/11/16808/#comment-109366*.

extremely low (I, for one, would use a one in a billion chance). By applying Bayes's theorem, we get the following estimate:

$$P(Nova|+detector) = \frac{P(+detector|Nova)P(Nova)}{P(+detector)}$$

Let's put this estimate into a table:

Table 5.1   Bayesian illustration

	Nova	Not nova	Total
Detector +	1^{45}	$\dfrac{999,999,999}{36}$	$1 + \dfrac{999,999,999}{36}$
Detector −	0	$\dfrac{35}{36} \times 999,999,999$	$\dfrac{35}{36} \times 999,999,999$
Total	1	999,999,999	1,000,000,000

We know that the detector came out positive, which means we are in the "world of the first row." Now we must assess the chances. The probability that the sun went nova is now $\frac{1}{1+\frac{999,999,999}{36}}$, basically zero. Bayes's theorem gives mathematical expression to the feeling everyone has that it is much more reasonable to infer the dice have come up with "two sixes" than to infer that the earth has ended. Following the same logic, I sequentially update the probability that parliamentary systems are much better. I use my own numbers just to illustrate this. The beauty of the method, however, is its transparency. The reader may use the priors he or she finds most reasonable and see what the conclusion is.

You may recoil. Maybe the probability that the sun has exploded is so low that the intuition of Bayes's theorem can be illustrative. But none of the issues we are dealing with are so skewed. Is there really any use in guessing, when faced with so much uncertainty? Psychologist Phillip Tetlock has been studying forecasting—understood in a broad meaning—for over 30 years.

---

[45]   More precisely, it would be 35/36, while the cell below would be 1/36. This does not change the results, naturally.

"We are all forecasters. When we think about changing jobs, getting married, buying a home, making an investment, launching a product, or retiring, we decide based on how we expect the future will unfold. These expectations are forecasts" (Tetlock and Gardner, 2016). Evaluating the effects of different forms of government fits the description of forecasts above.

Tetlock has two major findings. The first one, which made him famous, is that the average "expert" we usually rely upon is about as accurate as random chance. The other finding—more recent and less well known—is that some people who cultivate specific habits of thinking forecast consistently so well that they deserve to be called "superforecasters." Here is his take on how superforecasters approach the issue of uncertain probabilities: "Probability judgements should be explicit so we can consider whether they are as accurate as they can be. And if they are nothing but a guess, because that's the best we can do, we should say so. Knowing what we don't know is better than thinking we know what we don't" (Tetlock and Gardner, 2016).

In that spirit, I will proceed to the estimation. The first step of a Bayesian estimate is usually the hardest, and this is no exception. Before reading this book, what was the probability one would have assigned for parliamentary systems to be vastly superior than presidential systems? Surely, it would have to be low. As McCloskey (2016) notes, there is

apparently [an] inexhaustible list of materialist factors promoted by this or that economist or economic historian [for the Great Enrichment:] coal, thrift, transport, high male wages, low female and child wages, surplus value, human capital, geography, railways, institutions, infrastructure, nationalism, the quickening of commerce, the late medieval run-up, Renaissance individualism, the First Divergence, the Black Death, American silver, the original accumulation of capital, piracy, empire, eugenic improvement, the mathematization of celestial mechanics, technical education, or a perfection of property rights.

I should still add the hypothesis McCloskey favors—ideas—and, naturally, the one this text is about, parliamentarism.

Maybe the probability for parliamentarism is 5%, the standard for how improbable a result must be by mere chance to be considered statistically significant? One in 100? One in 1,000? One way to think of this prior is to imagine what would be the probability that an intelligent person in 1750 (someone without prior knowledge of any of the theories and evidence presented in this book) would assign to parliamentary systems being much better. One in 1,000 seems like a good, very conservative, start. To see how improbable these chances are, think that they are very close to the probability that the next time you play roulette, you bet on the exact number twice in the two first tries (1/1444, which rounds to 0.001). This low number conveys two intuitions. First, it is very unlikely that the constitution's organization can have such wide-ranging effects. Societies' outcomes are influenced by a great number of factors. Second, governments by assemblies *feel* doomed to fail. Most people are constantly frustrated by long meetings where no one can reach a decision, and most people seem frustrated with their parliaments as well.

Now we start updating the probability, with the contemporary countries sanity check (i.e., the observation that the vast majority of successful countries today are parliamentary). What is the updated probability that parliamentary systems are much better given that the welfare indicators are so superior in parliamentary countries?

Bayes's theorem gives us

$$P\left(Parl|\,contemporarysanity\right)=\frac{P\left(contemporarysanity|\,Parl\right)P\left(Parl\right)}{P\left(contemporarysanity\right)}$$

We need to think of how often we would find a result such as this one if the hypothesis were true. It seems reasonable to assume that we would very often find such differences. If this system is so much better, then this should be apparent. I assign an 80% chance of finding such results if the hypothesis is true. We now have all of the elements of the numerator, but we still do not know what the overall probability is of finding the evidence to support parliamentary systems. We can break the probability down and estimate:

$$P(contemporarysanity) = P(contemporarysanity|Parl) \times P(Parl)$$
$$+ P(contemporarysanity|NotParl) \times P(NotParl)$$

The only number missing is $P(contemporarysanity|NotParl)$. What are the chances that we would find such an extreme pattern if the hypothesis were false? We know that a high number of characteristics (geographic, linguistic, legal) also correlate with all good outcomes, which means we should not be that surprised about finding anything that correlates a lot with good outcomes.

However, the number cannot be higher than 50% because we have no prior reason to expect that all of these developed countries should be parliamentary instead of presidential (we have already discounted our intuition against parliamentary systems when we established the first prior). Also, good outcomes are related to many characteristics but rarely by this much. So instead of 50%, we lower our number to 40%.

Doing the proper calculations, we arrive at our updated probability: 0.2%. As mentioned in the introduction, any piece of evidence by itself would not be very strong. We now see this is indeed true, particularly of this impressionistic evidence we are using—0.2% is not very high. But the chances are *higher*—they have already doubled. With our new prior of 0.2%, we once again apply the theorem with more evidence. Now we use the historical sanity check evidence. The first continent to have rapidly developing countries was the first continent to have parliamentary governments, and the first countries inside of this continent to rapidly develop also were the first to have parliamentary governments. The reasoning is very much the same, so I will apply the same numbers: 80% chance of finding these results if the hypothesis is true and 40% if the hypothesis is false. The probability doubles once more and increases to 0.4%, still low.

Moving on to the informal theory, we have to think differently. Given the hypothesis, what is the probability of a near consensus by the political science scholars dedicated to the question? I would assign a lower than 80% chance simply because consensus in social science theory is a rare breed. I use 70%; however, given that consensus is a rare breed, we should expect it to be even more rare if the hypothesis was not true. Still, we can imagine that the visible better outcomes of parliamentary countries—which we have already incorporated into our estimates—could be behind this consensus even if there is no reason for it to exist. Let's assign a 20% chance. After the calculations, we jump to a 1% chance of the hypothesis being true.

Now I consider formal theory. Because of the mathematical form of these models, I expect them to be less influenced by the visible superior outcomes of parliamentary systems. First, any of the models considered in Section 1.1.2 are hard enough to develop already, as stressed by Myerson (1999). Second, the presidential system is a very reputable concept among economists, so we should not expect formal theorists to be inclined against it, particularly if they had a strong model. Given the heroic assumptions in the one model that pointed to benefits of the presidential system, however, it seems that models favoring presidential systems with reasonable assumptions are simply not available. I would assign an 80% chance of findings this skewed if the hypothesis were true but only 10% if it were false. Now the total probability jumps to 10% after the calculations.

The evidence for national governments is also heavily in favor of parliamentary systems. This kind of lopsided result is not so common in the economic literature. Papers on industrial policy, the benefits of democracy, trade, the minimum wage, etc. seem to disagree a lot more. With this, we repeat the above numbers: 80% chance of finding the evidence if the hypothesis were true and 10% if false. The total probability of the hypothesis being true is now 50%.

Now we look at the evidence from private corporations' governance, which is the strongest piece of evidence. "Presidential" companies are a non-existent phenomenon, and companies have the largest incentives to promote the interests of their shareholders (if they do not, they go bankrupt). When I translate this level of confidence into numbers, I would not necessarily expect such an extreme pattern even if the hypothesis is true, so we keep the 80%. But I would definitely not expect this pattern if the hypothesis was false—I would assign almost a 0% chance that companies would be better off being presidential. But considering the possibility that the evidence for companies might not be translatable to national governments (for reasons we do not know but are conceivable), I assign a 5% chance of these results occurring if the hypothesis is false. The total probability is now 90%. The evidence from local governments is also solid. We repeat the numbers for national governments: 80% for true and 10% for false. The updated probability is now 99%.

For completeness, I consider that, however convincing I personally find the arguments by Achen and Bartels (2017) that direct democracy does not have that much evidence in its favor, a general positive opinion of it seems to exist in the literature (Matsusaka, 2005). We then update our numbers once more to reflect this general opinion. If the hypothesis is true, the probability of this finding should be only 10% and the probability of this finding given the hypothesis is false, 70%. The updated probability is 90%.

This high probability after a Bayesian estimate is what I meant when I said that the combination of the evidence made the case convincing. The most uncertain number is the first prior, but even if we assign a 1 in 10,000 chance of the hypothesis being false for the "intelligent analyst of 1750," the final probability is 60%. This is still a very high chance. If, on the other hand, we assign a prior probability of 1 in 100 (which is still a very low chance and seems reasonable), then the final probability would be 99%.

6

What to Do

This chapter is much more uncertain than the preceding ones. While by now I am reasonably confident of the superiority of parliamentary systems (and hope you are as well), I am not nearly as confident as to how to make it happen and will not pretend to be. However, certainty in public policy is a vain illusion. If we had to wait for certainty to take any action, governments would not do anything. The reasonable approach is to apply to this problem the same principles we already rely upon when we are implementing—or advocating for—policies we believe are good. I hope this book sparks a good discussion and exploration of approaches. However, it seems that every time somebody hears this whole argumentation, they are often convinced that parliamentarism is better but still maintain an absolute certainty that it could never be effectively promoted. I would like to list some actions that are both low risk and could achieve significant results.

First, do no harm. This basic principle of medical ethics is applicable in every situation. As in medicine, the need for its repeated statement derives from how often the principle is ignored. For policy purposes, first do no harm implies looking for actions that are already being taken that are doing the opposite of a policy objective. Invoking this principle is not just an innocuous act of making an obvious statement without practical implications. On the contrary, there are several ways in which different actors in the public policy arena undermine parliaments (and representative democracy) and strengthen presidents (and referendum democracy). Let us collective investigate how public actors (international, national, and local), the press, civil society, and ordinary citizens contribute to this trend and how they can stop it.

There are also numerous actions that these same actors can take to promote parliaments and representative democracy. Representative democracy is a robust idea; once it catches on, it stays and spreads. But it does need some encouragement.

ACTION 1: STOP KILLING THE CONVERSATION BY CALLING FOR A REFERENDUM

One common reaction whenever someone proposes the adoption of parliamentary systems is "great, just run a referendum and country X can become parliamentary." This is odd in at least three aspects. First, a referendum can be the outcome of an advocacy campaign, but it should never be the starting point. If you run a referendum on any given cause before you advocate for it, then it will almost surely lose because of status quo bias. For that reason, people rarely ever react that way when policies they like are being discussed.

Some of the most controversial policy issues today are climate change, abortion, immigration, trade, the death penalty, a right to bear arms, and a right to free speech. When people argue over these issues, the response is not "let's have a referendum." People feel these issues should be decided on their merits by the existing institutions. Some may feel that when the debate over an issue has come to a mature stage and we cannot expect that more arguments will sway people either way, then there should be a referendum. But it is never a starting point.

The second reason why calling for a referendum is odd is that, unlike climate change, abortion, or gun rights, the case for parliamentarism actually presupposes that referenda are a bad way to choose anything. Clement Attlee, prime minister of the UK following World War II, called referenda "alien to British tradition" and "a device for despots and dictators."[46] Two of the reasons why presidential systems fare worse are directly applicable to referenda: Arrow's paradox and expressive voting. In this specific case, Arrow's paradox should not be a concern. I have argued that parliamentary systems are better than presidential systems for just about everyone in a given society; if people were all voting their true interests and parliamentary systems were as good as I claim, they should win in a landslide.

Expressive voting, however, is a major concern. The arguments in favor of parliamentary systems, as seen above, are complicated and can sound elitist without proper elaboration. Even if the reader agreed with the general point of this whole text, I'm willing to bet you cringed a few times. The parliamentary thesis I presented relied on some very unpopular (and "unpopulistic") ideas that 1) general population majority voting elections on issues does not elicit the will of the people (as per Arrow's paradox); 2) elected politicians are, on average, more competent than the population they represent; 3) rich countries are rich because they organize themselves better, not because they have exploited other countries (even if they have exploited other countries, as many did); 4) rich countries are not only richer but also enjoy an array of other good things that poor countries lack; and 5) the fact that corporations adopt arrangements similar to parliamentarism is evidence of the system's superiority, because the market is efficient at weeding out bad practices. Although all of these ideas are mainstream science, they are also unpopular. If the advantages of parliamentarism are not extremely well understood, chances are it will lose a referendum vote.

The third reason why insisting on a referendum immediately is odd is that the countries that did become parliamentary (or democratic, for that matter) seldom resorted to referenda when they made that choice.

---

[46]   https://www.telegraph.co.uk/news/newstopics/eureferendum/12177881/
We-cannot-trust-the-Europhile-elite-to-hold-a-fair-referendum.html

First, parliamentary systems evolved through time as mentioned above and elaborated by Congleton (2010). Second, even the countries that adopted parliamentary systems in a single event rarely resorted to referenda. Of all parliamentary countries in the world, I know of only one that held referenda on whether to have a presidential or parliamentary system: Bangladesh. Chile and Brazil, in turn, chose presidential over parliamentary systems. If it was illegitimate for parliament to assert their own supremacy without a popular vote, basically all parliamentary countries would have to be considered illegitimate. Given that the parliamentary countries are exactly the most consistently democratic, this cannot be true.

Maybe parliamentarism should still be approved even without a referendum. People who demand countries only adopt parliamentarism through referenda usually have no problem asserting that at least some values are not subject to public consultation. Democracy itself could have a hard time being chosen in a referendum against an authoritarian charismatic ruler, and the argument can be extended to just about any of the provisions of the UN Universal Declaration of Human Rights.

ACTION 2: IN A DISPUTE BETWEEN THE PRESIDENT AND PARLIAMENT, TAKE THE SIDE OF PARLIAMENT AS THE ULTIMATE AUTHORITY

Even people who agree with the idea that parliamentary systems would be better very rarely take a principled position of always siding with parliament as the ultimate source of authority (even if they may still judge a parliament's decision to be a poor choice at any given time). Most of the time, they support whoever they think has greater merit, or most often they side with the president if they like him or her and with Congress if they do not like the president. Last, these hypothetical parliamentarists may sometimes even disagree with the president's policies and be of an opposing party but genuinely believe that, given that the constitution is presidential, it is important for democratic stability that the parliament not rely too much on its constitutional prerogatives of controlling the president, such as impeachment.

But the way parliamentary government came into being was exactly through a progressive decrease in power of the parliament-independent executive (Von Beyme, 2000; Congleton, 2010). Even if most countries do conform to "pure parliamentary" or "pure presidential" models, as Lijphart (1994) shows, it does not mean that they necessarily, or even typically, switch immediately from one to the other.

Any policy you believe is important for a country should never be defended against the will of the parliament. First, these kinds of policies very often "do not stick." The lack of political support makes the policy appear to fail, which in turn may make the policy even more difficult to approve by the parliament and effectively work. Second, presidential offices are subject to deep changes from one year to the next. If you and a president support a policy that is opposed in parliament, fate will see that soon another president may implement a different policy, which you vehemently oppose, against parliament's will. Parliament works as a "policy-solvent", which has the added benefit of reducing the costs of policy uncertainty.

With respect to a supposed overuse of constitutional remedies such as impeachment, it is not clear why this should be a concern. There could be two kinds of objections, legal and consequential. From a legal point of view, most constitutions regulate how impeachments should happen, and they typically give autonomy for Congress to decide when it is applicable or not. As long as the constitutional process is followed, this should not be a hindrance. From a consequential point of view, I have just spent all the last pages arguing that the consequences of such a new equilibrium whereby a president may be removed whenever parliament understands it to be better are quite good. Any action that is both legal and beneficial to the people should not be used sparingly; it should be used as often as needed.

ACTION 3: INCREASE EFFORTS FOR THE PROMOTION OF PARLIAMENTARY SYSTEM

There is a lot of energy going into the promotion of democracy worldwide. Although a large share of those efforts are ineffective and even counterproductive, particularly military operations, many others are quite successful and do not violate the rights of anyone. The promotion of parliamentarism could very well emulate these initiatives. I should stress that my suggestions are never intended to replace the existing efforts for democracy promotion, only to extend them.

The following are examples of promotion of democracy that could be copied:

1   International standards monitoring. Entities such as the Organization of American States, the Organization for Security and Co-operation in Europe's Office for Democratic Institutions and Human Rights, the European Commission, the Carter Center, and individual governments regularly monitor elections wherever they happen. The transparency, predictability, and consistency of these initiatives make them reputable evaluators of fraud. Evidence (Roussias and Ruiz-Rufino, 2018) indicate that these monitoring efforts are effective where they are most needed, namely authoritarian environments.

    These same organizations could establish minimum standards of legislative power, both formal and effective, and they could engage in monitoring. Given the much smaller number of people who participate in legislative matters versus voters in elections, these monitoring actions could be effective even at a fraction of the cost of election monitoring.

2   Introduction of "Parliamentary democracy clauses." Poast and Urpelainen (2018) document how regional organizations of new democracies help promote democracy among themselves by introducing minimum requirements of democracy that condition their participation in these organizations. Examples include (Closa, 2013) the African Union, the Community of Andean Nations, the Economic Community of West African States, the EU, the Southern Common Market (Mercosur), the Organisation Internationale de la Francophonie, and the Organization of American States.

    Given how important parliamentary powers are, these organizations and others could establish similar "parliamentary democracy clause" that would suspend the rights of governments that do not adhere to minimum standards of legislative autonomy.

3   Inclusion of legislative autonomy in governance indicators for aid agencies such as the UN's Democracy Fund, which does have some projects that involve strengthening parliaments in some form, but these are relatively few and have relatively restricted scope.

4   Increase of research. The amount of resources devoted to research about democracy in social sciences is vastly superior than what is dedicated to understand parliamentary democracy. Researchers would do well to dedicate a much larger share of those resources to understand how parliamentary democracies come about, are sustained, and what threatens them. This could happen in academia, think tanks, and governmental and intergovernmental agencies.

5   Promotion in the media. Democracy enjoys a distinguished position in all media—the press, Hollywood, music, and social media. Parliamentarism, or the perils of presidentialism, on the other hand, are never mentioned. There are dozens of analyses of Nazi Germany that delve into the horribly anti-democratic nature of the regime, but we do not see a Linzian examination of the role of the conflicts between the president and the parliament for the Nazi rise to power. Likewise, media treatments of authoritarian regimes in Latin America rarely discuss the inherent risks of presidential regimes. Almost always, democratic reversals are attributed to elites who are particularly narrow interested. At most, there seems to prevail a "naïve Cheibubian" view, which sees the military as the exclusive driver of collapses of democracies and rarely acknowledges the constitutional crises that precede the coups.

A BRIEF CONCLUSION

In the introduction to his now classic book, After Virtue, Aladair MacIntyre proposed a striking thought experiment. Suppose that the study of the natural sciences is prohibited. Then, generations later, a movement emerges with the aim of reviving them—but by this point nobody has any scientific training, and "fragments" of books and articles are all that remain. What would happen next? According to MacIntyre, many people would begin using scientific terms and ideas in conversation. They would argue over "the respective merits of relativity theory, evolutionary theory, and phlogiston theory." But what it actually meant to do scientific research would remain ungraspable. "Almost nobody" would realize "that what they are doing is not natural science [...] at all."

This book is motivated by the following conviction: we have failed to understand much of European political thought during the eighteenth and nineteenth centuries in the same way that MacIntyre's imaginary individuals failed to understand natural science. We read authors such as Edmund Burke, Benjamin Constant, Germaine de Staël, François Guizot, Alexis de Tocqueville, and John Stuart Mill. We argue about how to properly interpret their texts and over the meaning of "liberalism." But we have forgotten the concrete, overarching project in which these figures all were involved, the one that made their thought intelligible. That project was parliamentarism.

For each of the authors just named above, the defining feature of a free state was that it contained a space for parliamentary politics—an assembly in which political actions were discussed and deliberated and in which executive officials were held responsible. (Selinger, 2019)

In this book, I describe the advantages of parliamentarism and show that all good things do tend to go together, and explaining this phenomenon through a single cause is more realistic than positing several causes. Parliamentarism is a great candidate for possible cause, and a long examination shows that the system really stands up to scrutiny. Informal and formal theories support this argument, and parliamentary forms of governance have been helping collective decision-making in all sorts of arenas, such as national governments, local governments, and corporations.

Instead of going over every argument presented here, I will make one last analogy. One of the most common metaphors to criticize economists is that they tend to only "look for their keys under the lamp." I would like to introduce a different metaphor: the lack of attention to the benefits of parliamentary systems of governance is like the teenager who insists on looking for his shirt everywhere in the house except for the place his mother told him it would be, because he has "already looked there." Look again.

REFERENCES

Abramson, S. F., & Boix, C. (2019). Endogenous Parliaments: The domestic and International Roots of Long-Term Economic Growth and Executive Constraints in Europe. *International Organization*, 73(4), 793–837.

Acemoglu, D., & Robinson, J. A. (2012). *Why Nations Fail: The Origins of Power, Prosperity, and Poverty*. New York: Crown Books.

Achen, C. H., & Bartels, L. M. (2017). *Democracy for Realists: Why Elections Do Not Produce Responsive Government, Vol. 4*. Princeton: Princeton University Press.

Aksoy, H.K. & Guner, A. (2015). A Bayesian Approach to Demand Estimation. *Procedia Economics and Finance*, 26, 777–784.

Allee, T., & Elsig, M. (2019). Are the Contents of International Treaties Copied-And-Pasted? Evidence from Preferential Trade Agreements. *International Studies Quarterly*, 63(3), 603–613.

Andersen, J. J., & Aslaksen, S. (2008). Constitutions and the Resource Curse. *Journal of Development Economics*, 87(2), 227–246.

Andrews, M., Pritchett, L., & Woolcock, M. (2017). *Building State Capability: Evidence, Analysis, Action*. Oxford: Oxford University Press.

Angrist, J. D., & Pischke, J.-S. (2008). *Mostly Harmless Econometrics: An Empiricist's Companion*. Princeton: Princeton University Press.

Aydogan, A. (2019). Constitutional Foundations of Military Coups. *Political Science Quarterly*, 134(1), 85–116.

Bartolini, D., & Santolini, R. (2017). Political Institutions Behind Good Governance. *Economic Systems*, 41(1), 68–85.

Berkowitz, D., Pistor, K., & Jean-Francois Richard. (2003). The Transplant Effect. *American Journal Comparative Law*, 51, 163.

Besley, T. & Persson, T. (2011). *Pillars of Prosperity: The Political Economics of Development Clusters*. Princeton: Princeton University Press.

Binder, C. (2018). Political Pressure on Central Banks. Unpublished working paper. Haverford College.

Blume, L., Döring, T., & Voigt, S. (2011). Fiscal Effects of Reforming Local Constitutions: Recent German Experiences. *Urban Studies*, 48(10), 2123–2140.

Blume, L., Müller, J., Voigt, S., & Wolf, C. (2009). The Economic Effects of Constitutions: Replicating—and Extending—Persson and Tabellini. *Public Choice*, 139(1-2), 197–225.

Bonchek, M. S., & Shepsle, K. A. (1996). *Analyzing Politics: Rationality, Behavior and Institutions*. New York: WW Norton & Co.

Brennan, G., & Buchanan, J. (1984). Voter Choice: Evaluating Political Alternatives. *American Behavioral Scientist*, 28, 185–201.

Brennan, G. & Hamlin., A. (1994). A Revisionist View of the Separation of Powers. *Journal of Theoretical Politics*, 6(3), 345–368.

Brennan, G., & Hamlin, A. (2000). *Democratic Devices and Desires*. Cambridge: Cambridge University Press.

Brennan, G., & Lomasky, L. (1997). *Democracy and Decision: The Pure Theory of Electoral Preference*. Cambridge: Cambridge University Press.

Brennan, J. F. (2014). *Why Not Capitalism?* London: Routledge.

Brownlee, J. (2009). Portents of Pluralism: How Hybrid Regimes Affect Democratic Transitions. *American Journal of Political Science*, 53(3), 515–532.

Buisseret, P. (2016). Together or Apart? On Joint Versus Separate Electoral Accountability. *Journal of Politics*.

Canuto, O., & Santos, T. R. (2018). Economic Effects of the Brazilian Constitution. *Novos estudos CEBRAP*, 37(3), 417–426.

Caplan, B. D. (2007). *The Myth of the Rational Voter: Why Democracies Choose Bad Policies*. Princeton: Princeton University Press.

Carey, J. M. (2003). The Reelection Debate in Latin America. *Latin American Politics and Society*, 45(1), 119–133.

Carey, M. P. (2012). Presidential Appointments, the Senate's Confirmation Process, and Changes Made in the 112th Congress. Report. University of North Texas. *https://digital.library.unt.edu/ark:/67531/metadc122211*. Accessed June 6, 2019.

Carr, J. B. (2015). What Have We Learned About the Performance Of Council-Manager Government? A Review and Synthesis of the Research. *Public Administration Review*, 75(5), 673–689.

Cheibub, J. A. (2007). *Presidentialism, Parliamentarism, and Democracy*. Cambridge: Cambridge University Press.

Cheibub, J. A., Elkins, Z., & Ginsburg, T. (2014). Beyond Presidentialism and Parliamentarism. *British Journal of Political Science*, 44(3), 515–544.

Central Intelligence Agency. (2019). The World Factbook. *https://www.cia. gov/library/publications/resources/the-world-factbook/index.html*. Accessed on July 18, 2020.

Coase, R. H. (1974). The Lighthouse in Economics. *Journal of Law and Economics*, 17(2), 357–376

Coate, S., & Knight, B. (2011). Government form and public spending: Theory and evidence from US municipalities. *American Economic Journal: Economic Policy, 3*(3), 82-112.

Cohen, G. A. (2009). *Why Not Socialism?* Princeton: Princeton University Press.

Cohen, M., Karol, D., Noel, H., & Zaller, J. (2009). *The Party Decides: Presidential Nominations Before and After Reform*. Chicago: University of Chicago Press.

Colomer, J. (2013). Elected Kings with the Name of Presidents. On the Origins of Presidentialism in the United States and Latin America. *Latin American Review of Comparative Politics/Revista Latinoamericana de Politica Comparada*, 7.

Congleton, R. D. (2010). *Perfecting Parliament: Constitutional Reform, Liberalism, and the Rise of Western Democracy*. Cambridge: Cambridge University Press.

Cornell University, INSEAD, & WIPO. (2019). *The Global Innovation Index 2019: Creating Healthy Lives—The Future of Medical Innovation*. Geneva: WIPO.

Cruz, C., Keefer, P., Scartascini, C. (2017). Database of Political Institutions 2017 (DPI2017). *https://mydata.iadb.org/Reform-Modernization-of-the-State/Database-of-Political-Institutions-2017/938i-s2bw*. Accessed on January 2, 2020.

Dal Bó, E., Finan, F., Folke, O., Persson T., & Rickne, J. (2017). Who Becomes a Politician? *Quarterly Journal of Economics*, 132(4), 1877–1914.

De Pleijt, A. M., & Van Zanden, J. L. (2016). Accounting for the Little Divergence: What Drove Economic Growth in Pre-Industrial Europe, 1300–1800? *European Review of Economic History*, 20(4), 387–409.

De Vries, A., de Vries, R. E., & Born, M. P. (2011). Broad Versus Narrow Traits: Conscientiousness and Honesty—Humility As Predictors of Academic Criteria. *European Journal of Personality*, 25(5), 336–348.

Deaton, A. (2013). *The Great Escape: Health, Wealth, and the Origins of Inequality*. Princeton: Princeton University Press.

Diermeier, D., & Myerson, R. B. (1995). Lobbying and Incentives for Legislative Organization. Discussion paper no. 1134. Northwestern University.

Dowding, K. (2005). Is It Rational to Vote? Five Types of Answer and a Suggestion. *British Journal of Politics and International Relations*, 7(3), 442–459.

Downs, A. (1957). *An Economic Theory of Democracy*. New York: Harper and Row.

Doyle, A. C. (2018). *The Adventure of Silver Blaze: Sherlock Holmes*. CreateSpace Independent Publishing Platform.

Easterly, W. (2001). *The Elusive Quest for Growth: Economists' Adventures and Misadventures in the Tropics*. Cambridge: MIT Press.

Easterly, W. (2019). In Search of Reforms for Growth: New Stylized Facts on Policy and Growth Outcomes. Working paper no. w26318. National Bureau of Economic Research.

Edlin, A., Gelman A., & Kaplan, N. (2007). Voting As a Rational Choice: Why and How People Vote to Improve the Well-Being of Others. *Rationality and Society*, 19(3), 293–314.

Eskridge, R. D. (2012). Municipal Government: Does Institutional Structural Reform Make a Difference in Local Government? PhD dissertation. Mississippi State University.

Falk, A., & Hermle, J. (2018). Relationship of Gender Differences in Preferences to Economic Development and Gender Equality. *Science*, 362(6), 412.

Finkel, S. E., Pérez-Liñán, A., & Seligson, M. A. (2007). The Effects of US Foreign Assistance on Democracy Building, 1990–2003. *World Politics*, 59(3), 404–439.

Fisher, R. A. (1958). Cancer and smoking. *Nature*, 182(4635), 596-596.

Frederickson, H. G., Johnson, G. A., & Wood, C., 2004. The Changing Structure of American Cities: A Study of the Diffusion of Innovation. *Public Administration Review*, 64(3), 320–330.

Freeman, M., Pearson R., & Taylor, J. (2012). *Shareholder Democracies? Corporate Governance in Britain and Ireland Before 1850*. Chicago: University of Chicago Press.

Gallup. (2018). Confidence in Institutions. *https://news.gallup.com/poll/1597/ confidence-institutions.aspx*. Accessed on January 2, 2020.

Gallup. (2019). Congress and the Public. *https://news.gallup.com/poll/1600/ congress-public.aspx*. Accessed on January 2, 2020.

Geiger, A. W., Bialik, K., & Gramlich, J. (2019). The Changing Face of Congress in 6 Charts. *https://www.pewresearch.org/fact-tank/2019/02/15/the-changing-face-of-congress/*. Accessed on January 2, 2020.

Gerring, J., Thacker, S. C., & Moreno, C. (2009). Are Parliamentary Systems Better? *Comparative Political Studies*, 42(3), 327–359.

Glaeser, E. L. (1997). Self-Imposed Term Limits. *Public Choice*, 93(3-4), 389–394. Greene, J. D. (2013). *Moral Tribes: Emotion, Reason, and the Gap between Us and Them*. New York: Penguin.

Ha, H., & Feiock, R. C. (2012). Bargaining, Networks, and Management of Municipal Development Subsidies. *American Review of Public Administration*, 42(4), 481–497.

Hamlin, A. & Jennings, C., 2011. Expressive Political Behaviour: Foundations, Scope and Implications. *British Journal of Political Science*, 41(3), 645–670.

Harford, T. (2015). *The Undercover Economist Strikes Back: How to Run, Or Ruin, an Economy*. New York: Penguin.

Holford, T. R., Meza, R., Warner, K. E., Meernik, C., Jeon, J., Moolgavkar, S. H., & Levy, D. T. (2014). Tobacco Control and the Reduction in Smoking-Related Premature Deaths in the United States, 1964–2012. *Jama*, 311(2), 164–171.

Hommann, Kirsten, and Somik V. Lall. 2019. *Which Way to Livable and Productive Cities?: A Road Map for Sub-Saharan Africa*. International Development in Focus. Washington, DC: World Bank. doi:10.1596/978-1-4648-1405-1 License: Creative Commons Attribution CC BY 3.0 IGO

Howell, W. G., & Moe, T. M. (2016). *Relic: How Our Constitution Undermines Effective Government—and Why We Need a More Powerful Presidency*. New York: Basic Books.

Ihrke, D. M. (2002). City Council Relations and Perceptions of Representational and Service Delivery Effectiveness. In H. G. Frederickson & J. Nalbandian (Eds.), *The Future of Local Government Administration: The Hansell Symposium* (pp. 213–229). Washington, DC: International City/ County Management Association.

Institute for Economics & Peace. *Global Peace Index 2019: Measuring Peace in a Complex World*, Sydney, June 2019.

International Monetary Fund. (2019). World Economic Outlook: Growth Slowdown, Precarious Recovery. *https://www.imf.org/en/Publications/ WEO/Issues/2019/03/28/world-economic-outlook-april-2019#Full%20 Report%20and%20Executive%20Summary*. Accessed on January 2, 2020.

Jensen, N. M., Malesky, E. J., & Walsh, M. (2015). Competing for Global Capital or Local Voters? The Politics of Business Location Incentives. *Public Choice*, 164(3-4), 331–356.

Jimenez, B. S. (2019). Municipal Government Form and Budget Outcomes: Political Responsiveness, Bureaucratic Insulation, and the Budgetary Solvency of Cities. *Journal of Public Administration Research and Theory*.

Kapstein, E. B., & Converse, N. (2008). *The Fate of Young Democracies*. Cambridge: Cambridge University Press.

Kinsey, C. (2006). *Corporate Soldiers and International Security: The Rise of Private Military Companies*. London: Routledge.

Knutsen, C. H. (2011). Which Democracies Prosper? Electoral Rules, Form of Government and Economic Growth. *Electoral Studies*, 30(1), 83–90.

Kohlscheen, E. (2009). Sovereign Risk: Constitutions Rule. *Oxford Economic Papers*, 62(1), 62–85.

Kreft, S.F. (2007). An Efficiency Comparison of City Managers and Elected Mayors. Working Paper 2007-02. Indiana University.

Lee, K., & Ashton, M. C. (2017). Acquaintanceship and Self/Observer Agreement in Personality Judgment. *Journal of Research in Personality*, 70, 1–5.

Lijphart, A. (1994) Presidentialism and Majoritarian Democracy. In J. J. Linz & A. Valenzuela (Eds.), *The Failure of Presidential Democracy* (pp. 94). Baltimore: Johns Hopkins University Press.

Lijphart, A. (2008) The Perils of Presidentialism: Juan Linz's Analysis and Further Reflections. Unpublished manuscript. Cited with permission.

Limongi, F. (2006). A Democracia No Brasil: Presidencialismo, Coalizão Partidária e Processo Decisório. *Novos estudos CEBRAP*, 76, 17–41.

Linz, J. J. (1990). The Perils of Presidentialism. *Journal of Democracy*, 1(1), 51–69.

Linz, J. J. & Valenzuela, A. (Eds.), *The Failure of Presidential Democracy*. Baltimore: Johns Hopkins University Press.

Linz, J. J. (1994). Presidential or Parliamentary Democracy: Does It Make a Difference? In J. J. Linz & A. Valenzuela (Eds.), *The Failure of Presidential Democracy* (pp. 3–87). Baltimore: Johns Hopkins University Press.

Linz, J. J., & Stepan, A. C. (1996). Toward Consolidated Democracies. *Journal of Democracy*, 7(2), 14–33.

Lomborg, B. (2017). The R&D Road to Development. *https://www.project-syndicate.org/commentary/research-spending-development-problems-by-bjorn-lomborg-2017-11?barrier=accesspaylog.* Accessed on January 2, 2020.

Lucas, R. E. (1976). Econometric Policy Evaluation: A Critique. *Carnegie-Rochester Conference Series on Public Policy*, 1(1), 19–46.

Luppi, B., & Parisi, F. (2012). Politics With(out) Coase. *International Review of Economics*, 59, 175–187.

Lurie, Y., & Frenkel, D. A. (2003). Corporate Governance: Separation of Powers and Checks and Balances in Israeli Corporate Law. *Business Ethics: A European Review*, 12(3), 275–283.

MacDonald, L. (2006). Determinants of Government Structure and Its Impact on Public Expenditure and House Prices. PhD dissertation. Florida State University.

Maier, P. (1993). The Revolutionary Origins of the American Corporation. *William and Mary Quarterly*, 50(1), 51–84.

Mainwaring, S., Shugart, M. S., & Lange, P. (1997). *Presidentialism and Democracy in Latin America*. Cambridge: Cambridge University Press.

Martinez, L. R. (2018). How Much Should We Trust the Dictator's GDP Estimates? Unpublished working paper. University of Chicago.

Matsusaka, J. G. (2005). Direct Democracy Works. *Journal of Economic Perspectives*, 19(2), 185–206.

McCloskey, D. N. (2010). *Bourgeois Dignity: Why Economics Can't Explain the Modern World*. Chicago: University of Chicago Press.

McCloskey, D. N. (2016). *Bourgeois equality: How ideas, not capital or institutions, enriched the world*. University of Chicago Press.

McGrayne, S. B. (2011). *The Theory That Would Not Die: How Bayes' Rule Cracked the Enigma Code, Hunted Down Russian Submarines, and Emerged Triumphant from Two Centuries of Controversy*. New Haven: Yale University Press.

McManus, R., & Ozkan, F. G. (2018). Who Does Better for the Economy? Presidents Versus Parliamentary Democracies. *Public Choice*, 176(3–4), 361–387.

Michel, J. B., Shen, Y. K., Aiden, A. P., Veres, A., Gray, M. K., Pickett, J. P., Hoiberg, D., Clancy, D., Norvig, P., Orwant, J., & Pinker, S. (2011). Quantitative Analysis of Culture Using Millions of Digitized Books. *Science*, 331(6014), 176–182.

Miller, G. (2011). *The Mating Mind: How Sexual Choice Shaped the Evolution of Human Nature*. New York: Anchor Books.

Munroe, R. (2009). Xkcd #1132: Frequentists vs. Bayesians. http://xkcd. com/1132. Accessed on July 18, 2020.

Myerson, R. B. (1999). Theoretical Comparisons of Electoral Systems. *European Economic Review*, 43, 671–697.

Naumann, L. P., Simine Vazire, Rentfrow, P. J., & Gosling, S. D. (2009). Personality Judgments Based on Physical Appearance. *Personality and Social Psychology Bulletin*, 35(1), 1661–1671.

Nelson, K. L., & Afonso, W. B. (2019). Ethics By Design: The Impact of Form of Government on Municipal Corruption. *Public Administration Review*.

Neumann, P. J., & Cohen, J. T. (2018). QALYs in 2018—Advantages and Concerns. *Jama*, 319(24), 2473–2474.

Nice, D.C. (1984). The Influence of War and Party System Aging on the Ranking of Presidents. *Western Political Quarterly*, 37(3), 443–455.

Niemietz, K. (2019). *Socialism: The Failed Idea That Never Dies*. London: London Publishing Partnership.

OECD. (2017). How's life? 2017: Measuring Well-Being. https://doi.org/10.1787/how_life-2017-en. Accessed on February 1, 2020.

Ostrom, E. (2009). A General Framework for Analyzing Sustainability of Social-Ecological Systems. *Science*, 325(5939), 419–422.

Page, L., & Pande, R. (2018). Ending Global Poverty: Why Money Isn't Enough. *Journal of Economic Perspectives*, 32(4), 173–200.

Parisi, F. (2003). Political Coase Theorem. *Public Choice*, 115(1-2), 1–36.

Persson, T., & Tabellini, G. E. (2005). *The Economic Effects of Constitutions*. Cambridge: MIT Press.

Persson, T., Roland, G., & Tabellini, G. E. (1997). Separation of Powers and Political Accountability. *Quarterly Journal of Economics*, 112(4), 1163–202.

Pinker, S. (2012). *The Better Angels of Our Nature: Why Violence Has Declined*. New York: Penguin Random House.

Pinker, S. (2018). *Enlightenment Now: The Case for Reason, Science, Humanism, and Progress*. New York: Penguin Random House.

Poast, P., & Urpelainen, J. (2018). *Organizing democracy: How international organizations assist new democracies*. University of Chicago Press.

Poguntke, T., & Webb, P. (Eds.). (2005). *The Presidentialization of Politics: A Comparative Study of Modern Democracies*. Oxford: Oxford University Press on Demand.

Pritchett, L. (2018). Alleviating Global Poverty: Labor Mobility, Direct Assistance, and Economic Growth. Unpublished working paper. Center for Global Development.

Przeworski, A., Alvarez, M. E., Cheibub, J. A., & Limongi, F. (2000). *Democracy and Development: Political Institutions and Well-Being in the World, 1950–1990, Vol. 3*. Cambridge: Cambridge University Press.

Reporters Without Borders. (2019). World Press Freedom Index. *https://rsf. org/en/ranking*. Accessed on February 1, 2020.

Ripley, A. (2009). *The Unthinkable: Who Survives When Disaster Strikes And Why*. New York: Harmony Books.

Robert, H.M., Honemann, D.H, Balch, T.J., Seabold, D.E., Gerber, S., *Robert's Rules of Order Newly Revised*

Roberts, T. L. (2015). The Durability of Presidential and Parliament-Based Dictatorships. *Comparative Political Studies*, 48(7), 915–948.

Robinson, J. A. & Torvik, R. (2016). Endogenous Presidentialism. *Journal of the European Economic Association*, 14(4), 907–942.

Rodrik, D. (2015). *Economics Rules: The Rights and Wrongs of the Dismal Science*. New York: W. W. Norton & Company.

Rossiter, Clinton. 1960. *The American Presidency*, rev. ed. New York

Roussias, N., & Ruiz-Rufino, R. (2018). "Tying incumbents' hands": The effects of election monitoring on electoral outcomes. *Electoral Studies, 54*, 116-127.

Sachs, J., Schmidt-Traub, G., Kroll, C., Lafortune, G., Fuller, G. (2018). *SDG Index and Dashboards Report 2018*. New York: Bertelsmann Stiftung and Sustainable Development Solutions Network.

Saha, S. (2011). City-Level Analysis of the Effect of Political Regimes on Public Good Provision. *Public Choice*, 147, 155–171.

Saiegh, S. M. (2018). Policy Differences Among Parliamentary and Presidential Systems. *Oxford Handbook of Public Choice*, 2, 380.

Selinger, W. (2019). *Parliamentarism, From Burke to Weber (Vol. 121)*. Cambridge: Cambridge University Press.

Shugart, M.S. and Carey, J. M. (1992). *Presidents and Assemblies: Constitutional Design and Electoral Dynamics*. Cambridge: Cambridge University Press.

Silva, T., Vieira, M., Araujo, V. (2017). Cabinet Rules and Power Sharing in Presidential and Parliamentary Democracies. Unpublished working paper. University of Espírito Santo, University of São Paulo, and Texas A&M University.

Sing, M. (2010). Explaining Democratic Survival Globally (1946–2002). *Journal of Politics*, 72(2), 438–455.

Stockard, J., Wood, T. W., Coughlin, C., & Khoury, C. R. (2018). The Effectiveness of Direct Instruction Curricula: A Meta-Analysis of a Half Century of Research. *Review of Educational Research*, 88(4), 479–507.

Stolley, P. D. (1991). When Genius Errs: R.A. Fisher and the Lung Cancer Controversy. *American Journal of Epidemiology*, 133, 416–25.

Sunstein, C. R., & Zeckhauser, R. (2011). Overreaction to Fearsome Risks. *Environmental and Resource Economics,* 48(3), 435–449.

Svara, J. H. (2002). Mayors in the Unity of Powers Context: Effective Leadership in Council-Manager Governments. In H. G. Frederickson & J. Nalbandian (Eds.), *The Future of Local Government Administration: The Hansell Symposium* (pp. 43–57). Washington, DC: International City/County Management Association.

Teorell, J., & Lindberg, S. I. (2019). Beyond Democracy-Dictatorship Measures: A New Framework Capturing Executive Bases of Power, 1789–2016. *Perspectives on Politics*, 17(1), 66–84.

Tetlock, P. E., & Gardner, D. (2016). *Superforecasting: The Art and Science of Prediction*. New York: Penguin Random House.

Tocqueville, A. (1838). *Democracy in America*. New York: G. Dearborn & Co.

Vlaicu, R., & Whalley, A. (2016). Hierarchical Accountability in Government. *Journal of Public Economics*, 134, 85–99.

Von Beyme, K. (2000). *Parliamentary Democracy: Democratization, Destabilization, Reconsolidation, 1789–1999*. Houndmills/Basingstoke: Macmillan.

Whalley, A. (2013). Elected Versus Appointed Policy Makers: Evidence from City Treasurers. *Journal of Law and Economics,* 56(1), 39–81.

Wible, A. (2018). Inflation of Conflict. In R. Arp, S. Barbone, & M. Bruce (Eds.), *Bad Arguments: 100 of the Most Important Fallacies in Western Philosophy* (pp. 280–281). Hoboken: Wiley.

Wilson, W. (1885). *Congressional Government: A Study in American Politics.* Boston: Houghton.

Wittman, D. A. (1995). *The Myth of Democratic Failure: Why Political Institutions Are Efficient.* Chicago: University of Chicago Press.

Wood, C., & Fan, Y. (2008). The Performance of the Adapted City from the Perspective of Citizens. *Public Performance and Management Review,* 31(3), 407–430.

Zingales, L. (2012). *A Capitalism for the People: Recapturing the Lost Genius of American Prosperity.* New York: Basic Books.

ABOUT THE AUTHOR

Tiago Ribeiro dos Santos has been a Brazilian career diplomat since 2007. He has worked with Western Africa, the United Nations, the European Union, and G20 themes in the Ministry of Foreign Affairs. He is currently a government-sponsored advisor at the World Bank Executive Director's office for Brazil, Colombia, the Dominican Republic, Ecuador, Haiti, Panama, Philippines, Suriname, and Trinidad and Tobago.

Tiago Santos has a law degree from Pontifícia Universidade Católica in Rio de Janeiro, a professional degree from Instituto Rio Branco (Brazil's national diplomatic academy), and a master's degree from the University of Chicago Harris School of Public Policy.

He is married to Marcela and is the father of Andre and Ana.

Printed in Great Britain
by Amazon

46996040R00087